Snakes In a School

Andrew Hill

Copyright © 2024

All rights reserved.

No part of this publication may be reproduced, distributed, or transmitted in any form or by any means, including photocopying, recording, or other electronic or mechanical methods, without the author's prior written permission, except in the case of brief quotations embodied in critical reviews and certain other non-commercial uses permitted by copyright law. For permission requests, please get in touch with the author.

Contents

Dedication i

About the Author ii

Introduction 1

Chapter 1: 1978-1982 Northampton, U.K. 2

Chapter 2: 1982-1992 Milan, Italy 24

Chapter 3: 1992-1996 Atlanta, U.S.A. 51

Chapter 4: 1996-1998 Paris, France 68

Chapter 5: 1998-2014 Antwerp, Belgium 71

Chapter 6: Zug, Switzerland 75

Chapter 7: Melbourne, Australia 78

Chapter 8: Netherlands 80

Chapter 9: Riga, Latvia 85

Chapter 10: Astana, Kazakhstan 88

Chapter 11: Taipei, Taiwan 95

Chapter 12: San Jose, Costa Rica 98

Chapter 13: Cairo, Egypt 104

Chapter 14: U.A.E. 106

Chapter 15: Dublin, Ireland 109

Chapter 16: Monaco 111

Chapter 17: 2014 - 2016 Kuwait City, Kuwait 116

Chapter 18: 2016-2018 London, U.K. 127

Chapter 19: 2018-2021 Central West Africa 131

Chapter 20: Central West Africa (cont.) 135

Chapter 21: 2021 Northants, U.K. 148

Dedication

This book is dedicated to my long-suffering wife and son, both of whom have heard my stories over and over again.

About the Author

Andy qualified as a teacher in Northampton, U.K. After teaching in two of the most socially deprived areas of the county, Andy and his wife sold everything they owned (which, frankly was not much at the age of 23) and moved to Italy to ski and teach English in an International School in Milan. After ten years and the birth of a son, the family moved to Atlanta where Andy took up a Head of School position. There followed a 40 year career in International education, which took Andy to Paris, Brussels, Monaco, Nice, Kuwait and Gabon (equatorial French West Africa).

As a school inspector, Andy has travelled throughout Europe and Eurasia, Australia and Taiwan, Kazakhstan and beyond.

Andy is now re-settled in the Northamptonshire countryside where his is a semi-retired English teacher at an international football academy.

Introduction

Snakes in a School is a collection of tales and anecdotes from a roving International School teacher, Headmaster and school inspector.

Andy Hill left the U.K. in 1982 after three years of teaching in Northamptonshire schools. The lure of the ski slopes North of Milan was greater than the temptation to be told exactly where else to go by a group of disadvantaged pupils on Northampton's famous "Eastern development estates" (of which more later in the book).

Andy subsequently spent over forty years as a teacher and later Head of School in the U.K., Italy, the U.S.A., France, Belgium, Monaco, Kuwait, London and somewhere in Central West Africa. He has also inspected schools abroad in over twenty countries.

The tales and anecdotes in this book reflect humorous incidents over those forty years. All of the incidents described in this book are true, with some exact locations and names hidden to protect the innocent, especially in all cases where Andy thinks he may be sued. The events outlined are mostly in chronological order; but should you desire an explanation for the book's title, "Snakes in a School" then you may like to read Chapter 19 first …

Chapter 1: 1978-1982 Northampton, U.K.

1978-1982 "Where's the f…ing St. Bernard?"- from Northampton to the Dolomites, Italy

Prologue

Episode 1- "Where's the f…..g St Bernard?"

In the beginning there was … the "Eastern Development", Northampton. This was my first teaching post. A middle school in the worst part of Northampton, the so-called 'Eastern Development'.

Meg, my first Deputy Headteacher and mentor during my probationary (first) year of teaching, was a hard lady. She was a tough Glaswegian. Hard as nails. In fact her shoe heels **were** nailed. Meg had nailed metal 'segs' to her heels. 'Segs' were crescent shaped pieces of metal, originally added to heels to stop them wearing down but Meg used them for a different reason.

'Click-clack, click-clack' went Meg's shoes down the school corridor.

"You see laddie, the hooligans in 5C can hear me coming. I don't have to shout to get them to be quiet, they are already quiet before I enter the room!"

I was never quite sure whether silent classrooms were a result of the segs or because Meg was the senior teacher who did all the caning! Yes, in the 1970's corporal punishment was still rife in English schools. Now, while I am against all forms of corporal punishment, I have to admit that Meg also used psychological punishments which many teenagers found worse than the cane.

Meg was able to feign anger in a way that made even the teachers terrified of her.

"Get in my office you good for nothing."

The terrified student (or occasionally the terrified teacher) would be escorted to Meg's office, whereupon she would slam the door, exit and leave them alone for hours.

"You see," she explained," they'll spend the next hour watching that door handle, waiting for me to come back, imagining all kinds of terrible punishments". (The worst of which, according to my class, was Meg calling their parents. Any amount of caning was preferable than parental punishment on the estate where the students lived).

Meg was so terrifying she managed to scare the daylights out of an entire ski slope, thirty ski school participants and four adult ski guides…

My first ever school trip as a fledgling teacher was to Andalo in Italy. The Italian Dolomites to be precise. Most of the pupils had never left their front gardens except to come to school. Most had vandalised the school or broken the school windows at some time in their illustrious careers- so skiing was, we guessed, going to be interesting.

The Italian Dolomites were a cheaper alternative for ski school trips from the U.K. in the 1970's. The main reason being that there was almost never any snow. On this occasion, there were very few slopes open when we arrived with our poorly dressed, poorly behaved and, well, poor state school hooligans. Meg had arranged the ski trip. I had not pictured Meg as a keen outdoors person. More often than not I pictured her as someone who drank Newcastle Brown Ale and smoked twenty a day.

Skiing in April was so limited that the accompanying teachers spent a good part of the day working their way along the hotel bar's top shelf of mysterious yet tantalising Italian spirits. The ski instructors looked after their teenage visitors (most of whom were more interested in swapping bedrooms at night time than skiing on mud during the day). Not Meg. Oh no. Meg, who had never skied before, went on the slopes to ensure impeccable behaviour was maintained.

"Robert, Robert Plummer!" Meg boomed down the valley. Ski instructors stopped, other school parties started shaking nervously, local inhabitants closed their windows and locked their doors.

Robert was a lovely boy. Robert loved his reggae. Robert was a Rastafarian. And Robert wore his Rastafarian, Ethiopian coloured woolly hat under his Afro hairdo. Unfortunately, Robert had left his gloves, one ski stick, a ski and one boot on the ski bus.

"Where do you think you're going dressed like a Jamaican on holiday? This is the Alps, it's freezing here. We're 1500 metres up in the air, you can hardly put one foot in front of the other in P.E. at school and look at you. Not exactly dressed like Jean Claude Killy are you? Get back to the hotel nooooooooow!"

The 'noooooow' echoed along the valley. Squirrels shot up trees, marmots ran into their holes, chamois deer left trails of liquid poo on the virgin slow, lynx … I think you get the idea.

Unfortunately, cheap British state-school ski holidays in the 1970's were so cheap that even the ski lift operators worked shorter hours. The effect of this arduous Italian working day was felt by Meg one cloudy day in April.

It was 4 p.m. Our group was back at the hotel and we were in the bar (third bottle, top shelf) waiting for Meg to join us. Leonard passed the bar. Leonard was a 14 year old who knew everything about the staff (who was going out with whom, who was married to whom, and who was having … well, again, I think you get the idea).

"Where's Mrs M? Did she not come down with you?"

"She's up the fuckin' mountain," offered Leonard. Our most reliable school informant (who was already practically on the payroll of the local Northants police).

"Are you sure? And there's no need to swear."

"Of course I'm fuckin sure, she was last on the chair when they switched it off"

"Well why didn't you say anything? And stop swearing for goodness sake."

"Had me caned last month, the ****in b**ch". Nah, she went back up the chairlift, she took the last ride up to check on Robert Plummer. Robert left his Rasta hat on the snow outside the ski store."

"What time was this?"

"Four o'clock. I remember because the ski lift operator said, "Chiuso, quattro"._

How Leonard learned Italian when he could not read or write in English was beyond me.

Unable to convince the ski instructors to start a search (yes, Italy 1979), Richard and I headed up the mountain. We trudged uphill about 200 metres shouting Meg's name till we saw a figure walking towards us.

Apparently, Meg was still on the chair lift when the operators decided to go home and switched it off. In those days ski lift operators were supposed to ski under each chairlift to check each chair was vacant. However, in April in the Dolomites there is frequently no snow under the chair lifts. Luckily the lift had stopped at its lowest point and Meg kicked off her ski boots, jumped out of the chair and made her way down the slope.

"Where's the dog with me whiskey then? Where's the fucking St Bernard?" Meg demanded when she saw us.

Episode 2 - "Are these your underpants Colin?"

Nailed to the blackboard. A pair of frilly knickers. Written on the board in white chalk, the words,

'Are these your underpants Colin?'

Sammy, our English teacher and local musician, had found the messy article in his classroom one Monday morning. His classroom was a temporary sort of hut, a 'mobile' as these were called. 'Mobiles' in those days were additional temporary classroom accommodation for oversubscribed schools. Sammy's was closest to the local housing estate and was frequently burgled. Local couples would, well, "couple" in the mobile at night, where it was warmer…

Colin was the school Casanova and claimed success with all the girls but we knew better. It was clearly time for Sammy to take him down a peg or two which of course he did. Colin suffered classmate taunts all day…

Episode 3- Parents' Evening

Later that term it was parent's evening. Our second Deputy (no, not Meg of the St Bernard incident) had been campaigning for the school uniform. The problem was that the school sweater was lemon yellow. Yes the Governors had somehow decided (or perhaps God had intervened- this being a Church of England school) to dress 14 year old estate thugs in lemon yellow.

A tailor's dummy was positioned in the school entrance, dressed in the regulation lemon yellow uniform and accompanied by a large poster which read,

'Your school uniform needs you', with the hand of the dummy pointing accusingly towards the school entrance pathway- presumably at guilty parents who had not yet purchased the obligatory yellow sweater. The Deputy, a deeply religious man and hopeless disciplinarian, had not counted on one of our teachers altering the dummy the night of parent's evening.

Dave taught PE and Humanities. But most importantly Dave had bought a house on the estate through an incentive scheme for valid workers. Consequently Dave knew everything about the families on the estate. Who the thieves were, who was having an affair with whom, drugs, vandalism; you name it. Dave knew what was going on, drank in the same pubs as the parents and was held in great respect by both children and parents alike.

Dave was also a great practical joker and had previously locked the Deputy in the toilet by taking the spindle out of the door handle.

On the day of parents evening, minutes before the arrival of the parents, Dave re-dressed the tailor's dummy. Gone was the yellow sweater (replaced by an orange construction worker's jacket), gone was the poster (replaced by a new one stating, 'Dress Like a parent')

The biggest alteration was the dummy's hand which had now been unscrewed from the arm and placed in the fly zip of the dummy's trousers with the fingers poking out of the zip itself. The parents loved it and the dummy was the talk of the estate for months. Everyone knew it was Dave, but such was the loyalty on the estate that no one snitched, and the school leadership were as afraid of the kids as their own parents were!

Episode 4 Estate Bonfire

It was Dave who stole the Guy Fawkes furniture later that year. As the main school on the housing estate, we were allowed to organise a communal bonfire night. During the day I watched out of my classroom window as a group of our school's finest thugs placed items of old furniture on the bonfire in the middle of the football field. They were accompanied by the school science teacher, clearly the staff expert in pyrotechnics.

Later in the day I saw the same thugs remove the best items of furniture and carry them, this time accompanied by Dave back across the estate. It later transpired that Dave had just bought a house which until November 5th was bereft of furniture …

Episode 5 A Parent visitor

My Head of Year, Dick, loved a practical joke.

"You have a visitor after school, a parent, Mrs. S, Caroline's mum"

"Why could she not come to see me at parents' evening?"

"Aah, she works strange shifts, does Mrs. S."

"Really, what does she do? Her daughter's never at school. In fact she's absent more often than she is present."

"Not sure, I think she may be an international lawyer or something…"

Now this was hard to believe. There were only two parents with above average education in my class. One was the shopping centre's pub landlord, and the other the school secretary. In addition, Caroline was as thick as a plank.

"So why doesn't she send Caroline to school then?"

"Says she wants her to become a model. She doesn't need school."

I waited. 4 p.m. no Mrs. S…

5 p.m. no show …

"Be patient, you will not want to miss her, she is *so* interesting, what with her working for Amnesty International and all."

At 5:30, an hour and a half late, a figure breezed into my classroom. In fact the perfume arrived ten minutes before Mrs. S. did. A beautiful woman, dressed to kill, make-up laid on with a trowel, voluptuous body, legs as long as … need I go on? Definitely not the picture of the international lawyer described to me earlier.

"Allow Mr. H, aw roight?" A broad cockney accent greeted me behind troweled on make-up. (Most of the parents on the estate were encouraged to move to Northampton's Eastern development from the East End of London because of cheap housing and quick jobs).

"Now then. My Caroline, see? You can slap 'er if she gets outta' hand Mr. H"

"Well I don't really agree with corp…"

"Ow old are yer then? You married?"

"I don't really see what that has to do with …"

"If you need a woman Mr H you just call me."

I could see Dick in the corridor behind Mrs C. moulding his hands in the air in the shape of a heart. Yes you guessed, Mrs. S. ran the local massage parlour.

Episode 6 Northampton hooligans visit Brittany

My second trip was to France. Northants county had bought a farmhouse in rural Brittany and the county's pupils would spend a week immersed in the French language. Unfortunately, ours spent a week immersed in pastis at the local bar. Winnifred, our English teacher, would evict them so often and with such force that even the local red-nosed farmhands would feel guilty and leave.

On one such trip, Andrew K, another school informant, was nowhere to be found. We had dropped the kids off in different villages and they were supposed to use their French to read the map, ask for directions, and make their own way back on foot.

Only Andrew K didn't. He did not make it back on time ... or on foot.

Around 8 pm - two hours late- Andrew drove into the farmyard on a French Mobilette moped.

"Oh my god he's nicked a French moped!"

"No sir, he lent it to me!"

I was about to bend Andrew's ear when a battered old Citroen 2cv van, straw blowing out of the rear window and what looked like chicken shit covering the bonnet, sped into the driveway.

"Oh no, now the moped owner's discovered the theft- that's all we need!"

The French peasant shook Andrew's hand, said "Bonsoir", loaded the mobilette in the 2CV and rumbled off.

I walked towards Andrew.

"Sir, before you kick off, let me explain. You dropped me off this morning, I went straight to the nearest farm and asked the farmer if I could hang around till 6, then I'd go back. He speaks perfect English, something to do with the Resistance whatever that is and agreed. He says English teachers always dump their kids in the middle of nowhere so staff can spend the afternoon in the bar. Is that what you did sir?"

"Well, we, er… never you mind, get in and get your dinner."

Episode 7 'Cock of the School'

The Deputy Headteacher had given me warning of a parental visit. A new boy was starting that morning. For some reason I suspected another wind up.

"Super kid, very smart, smartly dressed, clean, looks intelligent" the Deputy H assured me.

"That'll be a first. Our kids are usually scruffy, poorly dressed and thick as planks," I retorted.

"Ah, wait till you see this one, Phillip is on his way now.

Phillip was indeed on his way down the corridor, lurching towards me like a handicapped orangutan. As he approached I could see and smell the breakfast he had just devoured. Most of it was smeared around his lips and bits were stuck to his off yellow school uniform sweater. I could also smell Phillip. Everyone could. Even the lizards in the lizard tanks scuttle under rocks.

"Mr. Hill, this is Phillip. Phillip, this is Mr. Hill, your new teacher of English and Humanities."

"Phillip, what's your last name?"

"Tidy."

"Sorry?"

"It's Tidy, Phillip Tidy- everyone makes fun of my name."

"I can't think why," I replied encouragingly.

"Who's the cock sir?"

"I beg your pardon?"

"The cock, the cock of the school, the toughest kid?"

I could see where this was going. Under normal circumstances I would never condone fisticuffs between teenagers but I had a feeling it might be a good idea to make an exception. This kid looked like he needed taking down a peg or two (though this seemed to have already happened to his clothes- drainpipe trousers too short for him and the sleeves of his sweater barely arriving at his wrists).

"That would be Hosea, Hosea Singende."

Hosea was indeed the best fighter in the school. Hosea was a boxer at his dad's gym on the estate and Hosea was a huge Zambian kid with muscles in his spit.

"Whatever you do, make sure there's no fighting on school premises, and er, of course not during school time."

At 4:00 p.m. I gazed out of my window to see the entire school walk towards the far field, on the edge of the estate. At the head of the exodus was Phillip, just behind him was Hosea.

Phillip arrived late for assembly the next day. He had a large black eye and several bruises around his ears. I could also see the beans he had for breakfast, or at least the remnants of them on his cuffs.

"Morning Phillip, did you find Hosea then?"

"Fuck off sir,"

"Charming …"

Episode 8- 'Pit props Tommy' and Brian's fish

Part 1

In the late 1970's and early eighties the U.K. became home to a few new arrivals; immigrants from Vietnam, known colloquially as 'boat people'; though it was hard to imagine how they arrived on the shores of Great Yarmouth in a boat from Saigon…

Schools welcomed the families. Especially schools like ours. The Vietnamese were sharp, quick and often brilliant-especially at Maths.

Tommy was no exception. The only problem Tommy had was acquiring the Queen's spoken English. Our geography teacher took great delight in choosing super difficult words for Tommy to pronounce.

"Now class; the 19th century coal mine tunnel shafts were supported with blocks of wood called 'pit props' you see Tommy?"

"Pi-plop?"

"Pit props, Tommy, pit props, p…i…t…p…r…o…p…s"

"Aagh pi plo'".

Mind you, Tommy learned school English pretty quickly. Not exactly the queen's- more like the estate English at the Queen's Head pub.

One morning, Tommy rushed into class, clearly upset.

"He called me fo koh!"

"Now Arthur that's not nice- Tommy is not a fucker."

"No sir, two words, he called me f*****g c**t."

Episode 9 Brian's fish

There was no doubt that they were all dead. The tropical fish in some dozen or so fish tanks were all floating on the surface, staring at the wads of wet paper towel stuck to the polystyrene ceilings (yes, that game never ceases in schools across the country). These fish, mostly guppies and catfish with a few zebras, and neons, were Meg's pride and joy. There were fish tanks in every corridor. Indeed, we had fish, turtles, lizards (well one lizard, its mate had escaped between the library books, much to the amazement of the school cleaners ...) everywhere. Except there were now no more fish ...

"Who's killed ma' feeesh?" screamed Meg in her strongest, most fearsome Glasgow accent.

Brian, thirteen years old with the brain of a ten year old, looked sheepish. Brian was a sheep actually. The meekest, mildest teenager in the school. In the pre LGBTQ days the other kids called Brian, 'gay Brian'. Brian's dad was a local police officer who patrolled the estate at pub chucking out time. 'P.C. Brian's dad' was as tough as old police boots.

Brian loved his mum. He loved her so much he bought a new washing machine from the shopping centre opposite the school. We knew this because 'P.C. Brian's dad' came into school one morning to ask if Brian had nicked his credit card. Brian had. Brian had nicked the card, taken cash and bought the washing machine. When we told Brian's full story to 'P.C. Brian's dad', his heart melted. Not quite as tough as old boots when it came to his son then ...

"I ... I ... was cleaning out the fish tanks Miss but the air bubbles from the tank kept blocking my view so I ...".

"Ya switched them off yer greet lummmy !"

"Er, yes …"

"Aye lad, and that's the same switch as the water heater … detention for a week for you laddie."

Detention for a week seemed a mild punishment. Especially since Brian used to hang around during detention and hoover the carpets…

Episode 10 Goodnight Miss Knight

… or it nearly was goodnight. Gary, our local special school 'student trade in' (the trade in being that he spent three days in my 'normal' class of thugs and two days at the 'Special School' presumably where he learned to be, well, 'special'). Gary was not inherently bad, but he just couldn't control his temper, particularly if he felt aggrieved by unfairness and especially when unfairness was meted out by a teacher.

Gary had been smoking in the bogs. We knew this because we all heard the grilling he was getting from the Glaswegian Deputy Headteacher.

"Hello Gary, you okay today then?"

"Oh, er yes miss."

"Only yer seem to be walkin' with a wee limp in yer rrright foot!"

"Er, no I'm fine miss."

"...and you have a lump on the side of your ankle…"

"Shit, I mean no that's nothing."

Keen on continuing the agony the Deputy added,

"...and the lump is rectangular, that's weird, here let me have a look."

At this point Gary caved in and withdrew the packet of Marlborough cigarettes from his sock.

Later that day Miss Knight, a religiously large lady (ie religious AND large) with a soft heart and no discipline whatsoever had accused Gary of smoking again (probably on the basis of the original tobacco smell from the morning's episode). Gary blew a fuse. He screamed innocence, that he'd already been caught by "that Scottish bitch" and grabbed hold of Margaret. By the time the Head of Pastoral arrived he had kicked her shins blue.

Episode 11 Promotion

In their infinite wisdom Northants County Council decided to promote me after only two years in the job and just before I let them down by emigrating to Milan. In the early 1980's a teacher's first promotion was from 'Scale 1' to 'Scale 2' and often meant longer hours, a position of responsibility and two quid extra a month. Not to be deterred, I took a job on a new estate near the town of Wellingborough; a place even tougher than my previous post in the same county.

I made the mistake of thinking that being Head of Physical Education in a Primary school, where I was to teach a class of seven year olds, would be easier than my previous posting with teenage criminal gangs. It transpired that seven year old criminals were a lot tougher than teenage criminals!

Firstly, they burned down my classroom. Or rather one of them burned down part of my classroom. Gary was the guilty party. Gary was a particularly lawless seven year old whose father was in the nick for grievous bodily harm. I never did find out who was grievously and bodily harmed but suspected it might have been Gary's previous teacher so I made sure I was always nice to Gary. But despite this, Gary broke into my classroom while I was away on a field trip to Guernsey, killing the newts and other wildlife I kept in tanks in one corner of the classroom (a sort of living 'nature table' well, temporarily living as it transpired)... Gary also set fire to the paint cupboard.

Secondly, the school had a swimming pool which I understood from the caretaker was too expensive to heat and was therefore only used on rare occasions (mostly during the school holidays and then only during the caretaker's barbecue parties …). I changed this. As Head of P.E. I was keen for these estate kids to learn to swim. This might come in handy during the long summer months of foraging for bicycles in the local canal.

On my first inaugural day of swimming lessons, Ralph, aged 10 and a half, leaped over the pool fence, jumped into the deep end and screamed,

"It's fuckin' swimming!' at the top of his voice.

Only it wasn't 'fuckin' swimming'- Ralph could not swim. No-one had told Ralph he could not swim, not even, I suspected, his parents. If you had met Ralph then you would understand why his parents had not taught him to swim … I let Ralph splutter and catch his breath. I watched for a while as he swallowed water and kicked his legs like a drunken spider. Reluctantly, I fished him out.

Thirdly, as head of P.E. I coached and refereed the football team evenings and Saturdays. Most of the posh village country schools were terrified of estate kids. We played well, fought hard and kicked hard. Especially Jack. Jack was the captain of the under eleven team, and Jack was only nine years old. A Scottish midfielder. A terrier of a player who was a born leader … unlike his dad. Mr. Macguire had been in and out of prison most of his life. Unfortunately by a weird twist of fate, Mr Macguire was released for Jack's first team championship game. Equally unfortunately for me, Mr. Macguire's loud, obscene profanities could be heard all around the pitch. The profanities were largely addressed to the referee-me.

"Fuckin' never offside yer fuckin' beanpole of a ref! You twat …" I think you get the idea.

We won that game 7-0. The village kids didn't know what hit them. One of their dad's did though. Mr Macguire turned on him as he was leaving the car park it seemed. Mr Macguire was back inside the next day…

Chapter 2: 1982-1992 Milan, Italy

1982-1992 Mozzarella in Milan, and other tales-Italy

Prologue

After only eighteen months in my second teaching post in Northants we made the decision to leave England to go on a permanent ski vacation. My wife and I had realised that we had been to school, then college to learn about school as budding teachers, then we started school careers. We had done nothing with our lives since the age of eleven so we sold our house, our piano, our cheese plants (yes, this was the 1980's) and left for Milan, Italy. We chose Milan over Vienna as a ski centre because:

a) It was not German

b) Italians are friendly

c) There was no German food in Italy

We spent the next ten years in Milan, hence the larger collection of anecdotes below ...

i) The opening week of my first international teaching job in Italy ended in a trip to the local mozzarella factory after a few lessons studying 'Food and Drink' (what else in Italy?). Unfortunately on arrival at the factory we were missing one eleven-year-old boy who, it transpired, often showed up late. He was the son of a wealthy pharmaceutical giant and was rather spoiled.

The old school bus, driven by the infamous Sergio (more about Sergio later), pulled up outside the mozzarella factory and was followed a few minutes later by a large black Alfa Romeo. The Alfa had tinted windows but I could make out Andrea and his father in the front of the bullet proof vehicle.

Having just left England I was not really used to pleasant, private school students. I grabbed Andrea by the ear.

"Not only were you so late you missed the bus but you had to get your dad to bring you all the way here. You're in detention this afternoon."

"But that's not …"

"That's not fair?" Of course it is."

"But that's not my…"

"Not your fault? Then whose fault is it?"

"No, that's not my … dad! That's my bodyguard, Antonio!"

The car door opened, a huge chested man, with shoulders as wide as a brick layer's chest, dressed in a black suit and tie, got out of the car. I caught a glimpse of a leather holster under one arm, with a Beretta in it.

I quickly released Andrea's ear. Luckily, Antonio saw the funny side.

"Andrea no take a da school-a bus-a- he will-a be kidnapped-a- better this-a way."

Sergio the bus driver was doubled up with laughter. This was the very same Sergio who the following week came to my lunch table while my class was eating.

Our school canteen was in a church social club bar (yes, bar, wines, spirits and all). The children ate off billiard tables; each covered with a plank of wood and a starch-ironed table-cloth. All the school's bus drivers served the children their pasta 'a tavola' except on Mondays when Sergio collected his winnings and made his payments ….

Sunday was match day- Serie A Calcio- football day. Friday lunchtimes Sergio would dollop pasta on plates and take bets from the children on Sunday's matches. Mondays he would settle the bets with each form table, irrespective of which teachers were on duty and clearly ignoring any gambling rules concerning minors. The fact that the children were eleven years old, and took lunch in a Church social club did not deter Sergio. In fact Sergio was the mini mafia of Milan. It was Sergio who told me to go to the market to buy my bicycle- my first major purchase in Milan. The flea market was next to the top security prison which housed inmates from the infamous Red Brigade; and, as I learned later, bicycle thieves.

Once I had chosen a bike the seller wheeled it away as we haggled over the price. I thought this was just to show me the bike worked but once I had paid I picked up the bike to cycle home only to find my hands covered in red paint. The bike had been nicked a few minutes earlier and re-sprayed…you've got to admire the Italians.

ii) … and the Nigerians, especially those who are sons of Nigerian consulate employees…

After a term of teaching history and the French revolution to Year 6, we planned a trip to Paris. Thirty eleven year olds with a multiplicity of nationalities, taking a plane from Milan to Paris was always going to be complicated- little did I know exactly *how* complicated!

The group was divided into two classes. There were two Nigerian brothers, one in each class (though mysteriously clearly not twins as one looked about fifteen and the other eleven). The younger brother was nicknamed 'Tickets'. He was the purveyor and reseller of tickets to the Serie A football games at the San Siro stadium in Milan. All the staff who were passionate about football would contact 'Tickets' before Sunday games.

On the day of departure, we were checking travel documents at the airport. Neither 'Tickets' nor his brother had passports as they were the sons of a diplomat, or so they claimed. The colonel of the Carabinieri customs police did not agree.

"They 'af to av-a diplomatica passports," he insisted, "or they cannot leave Italia!"

The other children were mortified. For obvious reasons 'Tickets' was the most popular kid in the class, with children and parents alike.

"Sir he has to come!"

"What can I do?" I asked the customs officer.

He explained that he would let both boys through, and we would have to take our chance in Paris. He kindly informed me that he would be on duty at the airport in Milan when we returned.

A few hours later the flight attendant announced our arrival at Charles De Gaulle airport. The plane door opened and we were greeted by a female gendarme,

"Monsieur Hill s'il vous plaît?

"C'est moi," I reluctantly revealed.

"Follow me".

I accompanied the gendarme to the British Consulate where we were unceremoniously dumped and told that we would need exit visas.

"But why the British consulate, if the boys are Nigerian?" I asked.

'Ah oui Monsieur, but you are British and you are not leaving France without the boys' exit visa."

I spent the next two days in and out of the British Consulate, who prepared paperwork and sent me to the Italian consulate for the exit visa. I then spent the last day at the Nigerian consulate for more papers. The excursion to Paris was a three day trip. We did not see much of Paris but learned a lot about diplomacy ...

iii) Our new Primary teacher was shot in Milan. In the shoulder.

To be honest, he did claim that an air rifle shooting on New Year's Eve was mild compared to what happened on every New Year's Eve back home in his native Liverpool. Bill had arrived in September, his first overseas posting. He had moved to Milan to be closer to his partner - who lived in Paris. (Clearly Bill was not a geography teacher). Bill never really settled in Italy, he never really understood the Italians and spent a large amount of time buying stamps for letters to his partner, one a day. Even this was a frustrating exercise for Bill.

"Non ci sono piu!" exclaimed the post office counter assistant

"Sorry?" asked Bill in loud scouse English.

"We av-a no more stamps-a."

"Is this the post office?

"Yes, but no a more-a stampsa"

"Where can I get stamps then?

"Tobacconist"

"OK, so while I'm here can I buy 20 cigarettes?

"English humour? No!"

Yes, this was the teacher who was shot on New Year's eve and almost died under a broken chair.

It was (and still is) the tradition for Neapolitan families living in Milan (and presumably Naples too) to throw out 'something old' on New Year's Eve. A way of welcoming the New Year. This involved throwing out (from the balcony) old chairs, tables, cookers, tv sets, and anything else old. Bill had successfully dodged the furniture but not the celebratory bullets ...

iv) P.E.

Jim was our Physical Education teacher and a talented footballer. The kids loved him. His idea of a warm up for his PE classes was to have the children run round the edge of the football pitch while he stood in the middle firing footballs at full pelt in their direction. If he managed to hit someone (invariably in the head) the victim would be sent to the nurse's office. The Australian nurse was a tough character who doled out camomile tea when children fell over and grazed their knees. Indeed, she doled out camomile tea for every ailment.

"Listen you gotta fall over sometime, otherwise you'd never learn to get up would you?"

Paul, Jim's predecessor, would take Friday afternoon's off to go skiing or research another bar for our Friday night food and drink. On one such Friday we left him around midnight to find his way home. In those days drink driving was an offence as it is now, the only difference being that no self respecting Italian police officer would ever stop you. Or so we thought.

According to Paul, on this particular night he remembered being overtaken and cut up at 70 m.p.h. by a female driver but remembered little else till he awoke to the sound of the Carabinieri breaking down his apartment door. As the door opened both Paul and the police saw the smoke billowing out from the kitchen. The fire department was called and managed to save most of the apartment. Paul thanked the police for arriving in time. He had left a pan of baked beans on the hot plate and promptly gone to sleep.

"We were not here for the fire. We came to arrest you for verbal abuse towards the wife of the Colonel."

"What?"

"Yes, it seems you screamed at her on the motorway and veered towards her car".

"Well I guess since you saved my life I'll be happy to pay the fine!"

Paul had rented a ski apartment for the winter season and weekends were spent driving from Milan to Madesimo in the mountains for two days of skiing. Staff were often invited. Paul even invited a couple of mates from London, though they did not ski. Paul's best friend drove Paul's car to the village to hire the skis, but managed to slip as he exited the ski shop and broke his ankle. The story goes that the Lancia's roof was strapped with one pair of skis and one pair of crutches. To make matters worse, the same chap hit the sides of the narrow tunnels on his way down the mountain to the apartment. The ice in the tunnels turned the car into a pinball machine with the driver bouncing from one tunnel wall to the other all the way down the road. By the time Paul arrived in the village after a long day at school his visitors had been trapped in the car for a couple of hours. The tunnel walls had crushed the doors of the Lancia and they were unable to extricate themselves …

v) Club time

Friday afternoons at the school in Milan was 'Club time'. All the children would choose a club offered by the teachers, no academic classes took place during the last two lessons on Friday. The male staff at the Primary school (three of us) ran a Sports' club. Needless to say most of the pupils chose Sports and we were inundated with children. After a few weeks of this (and after observing the Knitting Club had three participants) we approached the Head to strike a deal.

"Can we have Friday afternoon off once a month?"

"I don't think that would be fair"

"Then we will choose another club activity, not sports, we thought of chess."

"Okay, it's a deal, take one afternoon off a month".

Every free Friday, the three of us decided to explore Eastern Europe (still communist at the time). The plan was to visit a different communist country and return early Monday morning in time for classes.

On one such occasion we hired a Hertz car - a Fiat Typo- and set off for Budapest. Apart from Jim and myself we were accompanied by two other teachers, Mark and David. We headed for the Youth Hostel at the top of the Citadel in Budapest. At 6 a.m. we arrived and looked for a cafe, after which we checked into the hostel above the catacombs in Pest. Not wanting to trust the yellow coloured milk, Mark chose to start the day with a beer.

At this juncture I feel I should point out that Mark was a narcoleptic. He would fall asleep in some of the strangest places and at odd times. We were used to standing close to him in bars and discos, ready to catch his pint before he fell over.

Saturday night was disco night in those days, even in communist countries.

Two a.m. in the disco - no sign of our narcoleptic mate.

"We'll check the doorman to see if he left", I suggested.

"Yes, he left, he come back to disco next door, he thrown out," observed the doorman.

There were indeed two discos next to each other. It seemed that Mark had left ours, had a kip in a ditch for an hour and tried to re-enter the wrong disco…

We searched the entire city till 3 a.m. Wondering if he had made his way somehow back to the hotel, we conceded defeat and went back to our rooms, only to find a sleeping beauty in the shower basin; surrounded by his own urine. Of course, we were left with no other option than to turn on the freezing cold water …

vi) Austrian petrol station escape

On our way back from the short trip to Budapest, Sunday afternoon, we were in a hurry. Sundays in Italy was Serie A football and we had tickets for the Milan game. (Our P.E. teacher was asked by the school's Parent Association what he wanted for his wedding present. He replied that an A.C. Milan season ticket would be handy- despite already being in possession of one.

Two of our party were especially keen to get to Milan for the 3 p.m. kick off.

We had stopped just over the Austrian border to put decent petrol in the hire car (we had been 'kangarooing' all the way from Budapest). As poor teachers we had worked out to the last schilling how much petrol we needed to get home.

David went to fill up and pay. David was highly organised, a 'Captain Serious' on all our trips.

"Do not buy anything else, we have no more money," I shouted.

Ignoring my advice, David bought windscreen washer fluid, a couple of Austrian schillings' worth. David had no money.

"Er guys, does anyone have a couple of schillings for washer fluid?"

"No," (in unison) we haven't, and we told you not to buy anything!"

David went back to the petrol station and offered to pay by credit card. The cashier went berserk, screaming at him in German. We had already revved the car engine when David came flying out of the petrol station shop,

"Go, go, go!" he shouted. We went.

vii) Casinos and brothels

The Italian language is one of the easiest to learn and to pronounce, particularly for us Northerners.

The hard "a" in 'grazie' is the same 'a' in 'grass' if you are lucky enough to be born in Lancashire. Posh southerners with their 'grar zie' and their 'lar te' (latte) are often misunderstood by Italians.

Admittedly the slight change in stress on one syllable may cause confusion. I remember ordering fish juice instead of peach juice and describing my house as having large tits:

Pesci ('peshi') = fish

Pesche ('peske') = peaches

Tetti = roofs

Tette = Tits

My second school trip in Milan was the annual ski trip to Gressoney-a beautiful village in the Val D'Aosta. Our bus drivers transported the entire school to an Austrian owned chateau (run as I learned later by a female ex SS officer- or at least that was how she treated the students).

On our way to the resort I made a mental note of the Casino advertised on a motorway billboard. Fast forward to dinner on the fourth day of the trip and my evening off duty. The school bus drivers were also at a loss for entertainment. I suggested we go to the local Casino and spend a few hours there.

"Ho visto la pubblicità per il casino,"

Translation (or so I thought) : " I saw an advert for a casino."

Driver 1: Spilling his coffee,"Che cazzo dice?"

Translation: "What the f_ck did he just say?"

Driver 2: "Ha detto che ha visto un bordello, cerca delle prostitute!"

Translation: "Says he saw a brothel, he's looking for a prostitute!"

Driver 1: "Caspita, dopo solo qualche settimane in Italia sa già dove si trovano les troie…"

Translation: " Blimey, he's only been in Italy a couple of weeks and he already knows where to find the tarts!"

A simple slip of the tongue, an incorrectly stressed vowel led to the confusion,

Driver 1: Translation, "Nah I think he meant Casin<u>ò</u> not Cas<u>i</u>no!"

Yes the first is a casino and the second a brothel. The drivers re-told that story for years afterwards …

viii) Boschey and teacher hire

Mr. Bosche, Van den Bosch or just Bosschey was a teacher legend in Milan. Even his hiring process was, to say the least, suspect. Bosschey had come to Milan on a football trip from a school in Trieste. Of course he could not resist the company of yours truly and wanted to know if there were any vacancies at my school.

"'Course, you'll need to be interviewed by sweaty Betty the head …" I explained.

"Sweaty?"

"Rhymes with Betty," I added.

"What's she like?"

"Sweaty ... Irish and deaf in one ear, though no one has ever worked out which ear it is, depends on her mood. Anyway, come and help with the annual school fete and I'll set up an interview."

Bosschey was a super fit specimen of a footballing madman. He proceeded to hump tables and chairs all around the basketball area where we were to hold the school fete in an effort to impress Betty.

The fete consisted mostly of auctioning Milan footballer's shirts, fresh fruit, free school lunches and, on at least one occasion, one of the cleaners-Lucia. Well, not her in person but her services ... er ... cleaning services to be precise. Though to be honest, judging by the salt stains under the armpits of her overalls I'm not exactly sure how clean Lucia really was!

After a few hours humping tables and chairs Bosschey fell asleep on top of the gym mats. He missed his interview.

"Where's that friend of yours? He didn't show up for his interview," Betty demanded at the end of the day.

"I think he was exhausted carrying chairs and tables for the fete, let me find him."

"Really? That was nice of him, just tell him he's got the job!"

Just like that. No interview, no criminal record check (just as well ...) no teacher observation (equally just as well ...). Ah yes, bring back the Eighties!

Bosschey subsequently furthered his career at the school by organising trips every weekend. He would quite literally take out a map of Italy, check a dart at it and wherever it landed, as long as he had not been there before, Bosschey organised a trip there. The kids loved him. The parents loved him (who wouldn't want to lose a spoiled, wealthy son or daughter for a weekend and go out with the spouse)?

'Let's see, oh it's landed right in the middle of the Apennines. Who wants to come this Friday for a hike?"

(The entire class raises both hands).

"Looks like it's settled then, wild boar here we come!"

Wild boar indeed. It transpired that on one of the walks the children were indeed followed by a wild boar who was protecting her baby 'boarettini' (I made that Italian word up). Bosschey, a seasoned survivor, was heard to yell,

"Right kids, start running, throw your picnic over your shoulder as you run, they'll stop to snuffle it which should give most of us enough time to escape."

"Should?" "Most?" I thought …

Viennese Waltz and Appendectomy- Austria

The Head of School in Milan was a great believer in school trips whether cultural, sporting, or linguistic. In fact, it was rumoured that one of the teachers would take a map of Europe, throw darts at various countries and announce the destination for the next trip on Friday afternoons. I was more serious. After a few weeks studying the Napoleonic conquests (and I don't mean Josephine …) I announced a four day trip to Vienna. I realise we could have gone to Paris, but I had never been to Vienna.

International schools all over the world often represent the International community and local expatriates. This includes the children of consuls, ambassadors, footballers, gun-runners, mafia, bankers and the like. On this trip we had the Belgian consul's daughter. To be honest she only attended one day, after which she was flown out after an appendix operation in an Austrian hospital. The appendix crisis was the least of our worries.

We had interrupted our journey with a visit to Salzburg; the Mozart museum and later Hellbrunn palace's water fountains. Hellbrunn (does that translate literally to 'Hell is burning' anyone?) invited my 23 students and three teachers to lunch, salmon sandwiches and a fizzy drink. Later the same evening we arrived at our hotel after a number of stops en-route to let a few students off the bus to be sick. We put this down to travel sickness but later that evening in the sumptuous Viennese hotel we realised our mistake. Twenty three students being sick in a hotel in six or seven shared rooms is no laughing matter.

"The hotel say they are running out of bed linen and that if this continues they cannot keep us overnight," said Alex, a seasoned school trip organiser.

"It gets worse," replied Joan, a new member of staff, "The Belgian consul's daughter is in agony, says her stomach feels like someone is constantly stabbing her. She needs to go to hospital.

"That will leave us with 22 students in seven different rooms with no bed linen and only two teachers to supervise," I reasoned.

"That would be one teacher," said Joan. "Alex has just dived into the toilets for a puke."

I made my decision. We would contact the health authorities and see if we could be hospitalised temporarily. The relief on the hotel manager's face was palpable.

"Vee 'af a quarantine hospital nearby, I shall call 'zem immediately!" (All that was missing from his helpful suggestion was a clicking of the heels…).

Joan was sent with Appendix Annie (later diagnosed as a burst appendix- she got there just in time) and we arrived at an arrangement of World War II Nissan huts- the quarantine hospital. Every child was tested incredibly quickly and efficiently and the doctor announced food poisoning, salmonella (thank you Hellbrunn).

"You vill all stay overnight, just to be safe."

Our short trip was thus made even shorter.

Food poisoning does not last very long and by the early evening almost all of the students were well enough to complain of boredom. Herr Dokter was not going to let us go till the morning. What to do with 22 eleven year olds in a quarantine hospital?

I organised a mini-olympics. The sports centred mainly around the following events:

1) Team pillow fighting.

2) Individual races- a) Jumping from bed to bed in a circuit b) Sack (pillow case) race

3) "Wheeling the phlebotomy trolley" (a relay; and don't ask me what a phlebotomy trolley is).

4) Quickest arm bandaging race (team event) and finally,

5) Racing the emergency resuscitation trolley …

We had decided during the course of the evening that the students could not possibly suffer a coach journey back and contacted our insurance company who graciously booked a flight from Vienna to Milan the next morning.

We arrived at Vienna airport and checked in. Twenty two tired, bored, fidgety eleven year old students lined up at the check in desk. Boarding cards were distributed and everything was going remarkably smoothly until we noticed two boarding cards with the same name and therefore, one student was without a boarding card.

The check in assistant was already stressed because I insisted we sit together in order to have some control over our students.

"Sir, I cannot issue another boarding card, you are already checked in."

'Here we go', I thought, 'This is where Austrian rule observing meets Italian rule bending.'

"But there's no real issue is there? We have 22 students, 22 boarding cards and 22 seats."

"Yes, sir, but the problem is that the passport or I.D. card for that student will not match the boarding card."

I was tired, irritable and so were 22 students sitting on the floor in front of the desk.

"But there is no issue on your side is there? On my side we have a big problem. I cannot leave one student here with one teacher to supervise twenty one others all the way to Milan."

"Sir, zat is zee immigration rule …"

At this point I could feel twenty one pairs of eyes watching me. I even overheard a student whisper to his friend,

"This should be interesting. That assistant doesn't know Mr. Hill like we do!"

I stared at the check in assistant squarely in the eyes.

"Here's what is going to happen. I shall instruct these kids, on my count of three, to scream, cry and sob. Then, on my command, they will shout, "We want our mums," in unison and start throwing their bags in the air.

"Yeeeees," screamed the kids, 'go for it Hilly!"

The Austrian assistant started to sweat. His face flushed. He shook. I could almost see the inner turmoil in his law-abiding brain.

He caved in.

"Ah zo, as you say in English, 'on your head be it'! Go!"

There was a chorus of disappointment, followed by cheers from the twenty two behind me.

Red Cross-Croatia and rugby party- Treviso

The school in Milan had a large Yugoslav community. At the start of the war in 1991 Slovenia, on the border with Trieste, had already gained independence. Our school community was concerned that children and families from Croatia were flooding into Trieste in search of food and medical supplies. Naturally, international parents wanted to galvanise the school into action but of course it was too early in the Baltic war to take sides.

As a gesture of support myself, the PE teacher, a Primary school teacher and an ex-student decided to contact the Red Cross in Trieste. Peter, the ex-student, was a photographer and his brother worked for American express identifying hotels for Amex card holders. Both had transferred to the school in Milan from a state school in sunny Peterborough and had adapted really well to Italy. Accomplished skiers, adventurous and excellent students all round. The younger brother Pete was to be our official photographer. Jim and I were the drivers and Bosschey (a Belgian-Brit with a penchant for kicking the opposition in our 5 a side team) was to be, well just Bosschey.

Without much thought we rented a small truck from Hertz and set off to meet the Red Cross agent in Trieste. We had loaded the truck with antibiotics, soap powder and pasta; these being the three necessities at the start of a war. We used Primary school ribbon tape (red) to form a large red cross on the side of the van. Our thinking was that once we arrived in Trieste the real Red Cross would be emblazoned on the truck. Not so, the lady in charge said we had done a fine job and no more was needed.

The Trieste Red Cross representative to Croatia and Slovenia was a fearsome mighty mouse of a lady. Signora Croce Rossa was organised, disciplined and very military.

"Have you been to Rijeka before?" she demanded whilst looking at the five stooges in front of her.

"Er, yes, as a tourist I drove the coastal road all the way to Dubrovnik," I answered.

This was a while back on a truly delightful sailing and camping holiday with my wife.

"Well, we do not know how the road is, if it is dangerous and how long it will take to get to Rijeka, where we will meet the mayor and deliver the supplies. You are the first Red Cross truck into Slovenia and Croatia.

We were alarmed. For some reason we thought the Red Cross would be sending supplies daily. Worse still, the truck had four seats, there were five of us so we naturally sent Bosschey in the back where during the journey bags of pasta and antibiotic needles fell haplessly on his head.

At the Italian/Slovenian border we were instructed not to bring anything back from Croatia.

"The truck must be empty," insisted both Signora Croce Rossa and the customs officer; an imposing giant of a man in full Carabinieri uniform and with a chest full of medals. (Though to be honest I could not remember the last time Italy had won any wars …).

'What does he think we will bring back?"

"Children, bambini of course- everyone wants to save them."

I hesitated to use the phrases' coal from Newcastle' or 'busman's holiday'.

"Of course, we understand."

We crossed the border, promptly sent postcards from the Slovenian sides to our families and proceeded along the coastal road south to the port of Rijeka.

We had not visualised the new and very temporary Slovenian/Croatian border. It was a hastily contracted collection of old huts, bike sheds and very large concrete tank traps. It also concealed an area of mined ground, much to the consternation of our photographer who had ventured out of the van to take photos. On hearing the manic shouting of the border guards he nipped rather gingerly back into the truck.

The return journey to Trieste from Rijeka, where we deposited the supplies, were toasted by the mayor and slept overnight, was equally eventful.

As we crossed the border into Trieste the Italian Carabinieri demanded the usual documents: Passports and driving licence. At the wheel was our P.E. teacher . He leaned over towards me and whispered surreptitiously,

"The cops took my licence last week, speeding fine."

We were invited to step out of the vehicle while the Carabinieri Colonel, medals on chest, explained what would happen next. He would impound the vehicle, and keep it until the Milan police could prove the existence of the licence.

"This is a rented van, sir, you cannot impound it. What's the alternative?"

"Tuo amico passera la notte in prigione."

"What did he say?" asked the P.E. teacher.

"He said you're nicked," I replied.

Luckily Signora Croce Rossa intervened, screamed at the Colonel, tore up his record of the incident and probably told him she knew where he lived, who his mother was, and what might happen to him if he arrested any one of us.

On the way back to Milan, we took a detour via Treviso to see some Rugby mates. Treviso is the home of Benetton- sweaters and rugby team. It was a long winding journey up the mountains and we had totally forgotten about Boscchey in the back of the truck. On arrival at the party, around 11:30 p.m. we opened the back of the truck. There was a putrid stench of uri

"You bastards, I've been banging on the side of the truck for hours, I needed a pee!"

"Are those your shoes Bosschey, why are they soaking wet?"

"Where else could I pee?"

We took the elevator to the apartment where the party was in full swing. That is until the neighbour arrived at midnight screaming from the corridor outside. You can imagine his reaction when the door opened and he was confronted by the Benetton front row of burly Italians and Scottish prop forwards.

Chapter 3: 1992-1996 Atlanta, U.S.A.

1992-1996: Sue me, sue you - Atlanta-USA

Prologue

I spent four glorious years as a Head of Primary (my first Headship) in Atlanta, culminating in the 1996 Olympic games (G.B.'s worst medal haul by the way). A portent of those four years (apart from G.B.'s miserable medal tally) was my first day of school for new students. I was accused of kidnapping a child. Honestly you could write a book...

Incident #1- Kidnapping the Kid

Orientation day for new students should have been a gradual, calm and comforting introduction to school life for both new students and staff. Ah well ...

At the end of a successful day my secretary, a lovely old Atlanta born and raised lady who could test the temperature of my office from the other end of the campus knocked on my door.

"Sir, there's an iraaate and ah mee-yan ahrate gentleman who cannot find his child." Try to say this in a Southern drawl- think Rod Steiger in The Heat of the Night.

"Show him in." Me, so British accent of course ...

The father explained that his child had not yet arrived home, where was he? He had custody that day, not his wife but his child was nowhere to be found. He called the local police officer who was on his way.

A quick look at the file proved that Monday was indeed custody day for the divorced father, an Albanian American taxi driver who apparently was studying law and married to a local Giorgian W.A.S.P. (White Anglo Saxon Protestant as the Deep South liked to call this kind of lady). My instinct told me I could not be held responsible.

"Sir, your child has not been kidnapped. Officer, the child's mother has probably got her days mixed up, this not being an official school day, and has collected the child herself."

Charlie, our local school liaison officer and crossing the street patrolman was not happy at this parent wasting his time and left the office,

"Ah bid y'all a good day and you sir, y'all need to think agin afore you waste mah tahm."

I spent the next year in court because of this family. In the interest of time I'll skip to the end, one year later …

It is understandable in Albanian culture (and many other cultures too) that the only son of a family is the most important 'possession' a father can have. This parent took the cultural norm to the nth degree. He was fighting for sole custody of his son, not the 50/50 arrangements under the terms of his divorce. Unfortunately the most reliable source of evidence in almost all child custody cases is often the child's school. School's keep attendance and behaviour records, uniform rules, and observe general well-being. Whenever there was a problem with the child, it was usually the day after the father's custody day. Missing P.E. kit, an empty lunch box, no homework or absence.

I was called to the family court in the leafy (Peach-tree leafy) suburb of Marietta, a few miles north of Atlanta. Father was trying for the third time to gain sole custody of the child. The judge was a black, spectacled old lady, Giorgia born and bred. The case was delayed to 4 p.m. and I was anxious for my son who was being cared for by my secretary, alongside his new found friend (yes you guessed, an Albanian American child of divorced parents; say no more).

The judge wanted a little information on my background. I explained I was the Elementary principal at the International school, that I was British and that my son attended school in the same class as the plaintiff's son.

"Y'all have any minorities at y'all's school Mr Heeeel?" She had a beautiful southern accent, the kind that manages to squeeze three syllables out of a mono-syllabic word and make it last a lifetime. 'Hill' became 'Heeeeel' as it eased out of her mouth.

"Well, your honour, my son is a minority being one of only three Brits in the entire school."

"Mr. Heel let me explain, in the U.S. ah am not 'your honour' but thank y'all for the compliment. Secondly, bah mahnority I meant, well ... come to think of it, it *is* a mathematical expression so ah wheee 'yal staaand corrected!"

The judge asked me if I had met the father before and when I had first met him. I explained the event of my first day in the office and that he had used vulgar language to my secretary who had called the police herself. Judge Doris Day (my name for her) was intrigued as to what language was used.

"He said he would sue my arse maam ..."

"Y'all's whaat?"

"Er ass, maam."

"For such a profane word y'all say it so naaaaahsly (nicely). May I ask Mr. Heel, given that it's now 4:30 p.m. where is your child and who is caring for him?"

"He is with the plaintiff's son. They have become friends and since I never know which parent is collecting on which day it is safer to keep him in my office till pick-up time maam."

Judge Doris glared at the father beneath her half-rimmed spectacles.

"Now sir you have maintained that your son has had an excellent attendance record at school. Can you all confirm thayat Mr. Heel?"

"Yes and no. Excellent after mother has had custody and less so when father has had custody. Late to school the day after, no sports clothes, lunch box often empty. My son shares his lunch."

The father took out his notes and relayed to the judge the attendance days he had on record.

"Do y'all concur with this attendance record, Mr Heel?"

"No ma'am, the plaintiff has the wrong year, he is quoting from the year before the divorce I believe."

Judge Doris suddenly became the hanging judge of the 19th century. She glared again at the father, grabbed the gavel hammer and slammed it down.

"Officer of the court, take this man down to the holding cell, charge him with wasting the court's time, fine him a suitable amount and keep him there for three days."

Turning to me she continued,

"Mr Heel, the State of Georgia and the Family Court of Marietta thank you for y'all's taaaaahm, you may leave."

Doris (no longer a judge to me but a friend for life) added the syllables to the word "taaaaahm" (time) as if to give me a good send off.

Incident #2- The kidnapped kid's mom at the World Cup semi-final in New Jersey

I have related this story countless times to friends and relatives and all have had the same reaction, "That's just not possible!" But yes, I met the mother of the custodial child for the first time six months after Judge Doris sent the father down.

The soccer World Cup was in the USA in 1994. My best friend Nicholas in Atlanta was an insurance adjuster and had worked for a New Senator on a claim. The Senator was a keen follower of soccer and had even invented a board game which he asked me to trial at my International School. It was really crap but on the strength of Nick's insurance and my footie game we had been promised tickets to Italy v Bulgaria at Giants stadium, New Jersey.

The only problem on arrival was Nick's organisation. He had omitted a vital detail, the tickets ...

Senator X was holding the tickets and had asked Nick to collect them from him. Only Senator X was hosting the Irish team's leaving party in the VIP suites of the Giants' stadium. How would we gain access without an invite?

We tried the elevator to the top floor and were confronted by four bodyguards looking down at us; two scrawny pale Brits in M and S suits.

"Passes?"

We showed our stadium passes.

"No, your VIP invite pass *as well* as your stadium pass, please"

We got back in the elevator. Nick suggested we watch VIP s going up to see what extra pass they showed. Simple, a red dot on the stadium pass was all. A pair of scissors, a red piece of paper cut from a magazine and some Pritt glue did it.

We returned to the VIP suite, the bodyguards let us pass and were handed our tickets to our seats. No sooner had we sat when ...

A tap on the shoulder. A woman introduced herself. Yes, the mother of the custody case student back in Atlanta.

"You must think I'm haunting you."

"Too right I do, maam."

The mother explained that she had won her case to maintain 50/50 custody with her ex and it was all thanks to me.

"Two beers would be much appreciated at this point," I ventured.

"Coming right up!"

Incident #3 Car Pool Champagne

In the 1990's a well-publicised divorce settlement between two parents at the school became one of the largest alimony cases in the USA. Father had a number of I.T. companies and mother, well, mother was mother. Mother, Ms. H, did carpool like no other parent at the school.

Car pool in the USA is essentially a line of vehicles dropping off children at school in the morning and collecting them in the afternoon. I had organised the procedure in the best British fashion. For pick up, cars displayed numbers in their windscreens, children sat under their number in the school gym, students armed with walkie-talkies called the numbers in to me and I sent the students out to their respective cars. Clockwork.

The morning was less hectic as parents arrived between 08:00 a.m. and 08:45 a.m. and had plenty of time to stop and drop off. The tradition at the school was for the Senior leaders to open the car doors, say hip to mostly dads, and pass the time of day,

"Morning, homework and sports kit in the bags? Out you come, enjoy your day sir."

I used to thoroughly enjoy morning drop off. It was always a pleasant occasion, I mean dads dropping off their kids for the day was the only time we saw most of these high-powered executives. Only Ms. H did carpool her way. The girls would be in the back of a limo, eating cereal out of the box. Remember those Variety packs of cereal you could tear the side off and pour the milk in directly to save time and washing up? Well, Ms. H was certainly not into washing up … Ms. H was into partying after the divorce. Ms. H barely had time to get the kids dressed in the morning with the girls often holding up drop off as they finished breakfast in the back of the limo.

One morning was particularly memorable. The limo pulled up. I saw the kids in the back eating breakfast and opened the door as the vehicle approached the drop off sign

"Good morning," I had barely finished the word, 'morning' when, as I opened the door to let the children out, a champagne glass rolled onto the school kerb with an expensive 'tinkle' and the remnants of Moet Chandon spilling on my shoe.

"Have a good night last night did we?" I asked.

"Mr. Heel, only a skooowell principal from England could aks me a question laaak dayat!"

The three syllables added to the word 'school' and the Southern Georgia drawl of 'that' were music to my ears.

Incident #4 1996 Atlanta Olympics' Aussie Bar

During the 1996 Atlanta Olympic year I had the honour of representing Malta as their 'Olympic Envoy' (basically their gofer, providing transport, drivers, passes and tickets. (More of Malta later).I was also asked to raise money, through the school's connections, for the B.O.C. British Olympic Committee. The money was used to provide transport and hospitality for the athletes' family members, and to build a British style pub near the Georgia Tech University campus for large screening of the events. Early in 1996 I had met two Aussie beer entrepreneurs who were trying to break into the beer desert known locally as the 'Budweiser monopoly'. Yes, two Australains in the U.S. deep south were bringing their own locally brewed version of Aussie lager and needed P.R. events to advertise their brews. As the school had hosted frequent Olympic Envoy events during the run up to Atlanta 1996 it was fitting that I should volunteer the use of the school hall and music room. This was the same music room I had discovered on my arrival at the school in 1992 with more windows on the outside than on the inside, due to the fact that our Irish American caretaker had built himself an apartment at one end, practically inside the instrument storage cupboard.

The Aussie beer event coincided with a B.O.C. fundraiser and Olympic Envoy meeting. The morning after the event the Aussie beer guys were supposed to arrive early to clean up and dismantle the bar they had created (along with Aussie paraphernalia- roos, wombats and the like strung up across the school hall). Unfortunately the event also coincided with the school's Open Day- an event I had somehow missed when checking my calendar a few months earlier.

By 10:00 a.m. on Saturday morning the school hall and music room smelled heavily of hops, malt and Australians. Aussie beer craftsmen were nowhere to be seen. I assumed they had not yet drunk enough of their own lager to get used to the alcohol levels, (6.8) and were having a lie in or walkabout. Luckily, Joe and Mary, the school cleaners were called and were more than happy for the overtime. Joe and Mary cleaned my office for four years and during that entire time I did not understand a single word they said to me; their heavy Southern drawl being completely unintelligible. The B.O.C. were grateful for the funds raised and presumably used the money to celebrate the only gold medal we won in Atlanta 1996: Redgrave and Pinsent of course in the rowing.

As Olympic envoy for Malta I had countless adventures and spent the summer holidays of 1996 living in the Olympic Village at Georgia Tech and travelling to the beautiful city of Savannah where the Olympic sailing was held. Mind you Malta's windsurfer, a young Scottish-Maltese falcon, was less than impressed with the sailing. Having spent all his life in the calm waters of the Med, he was not prepared for a full scale tornado warning in Savannah harbour!

Incident #5 PE teacher interview

"Evenin' y'all ma nayem is Salleeee ahl be y'all's waitress fo' this even-in."

A pizzeria in the Atlanta suburbs was not the ideal venue for an interview but we had rejected twenty candidates that afternoon and were becoming desperate. Sally, the waitress, was working as late as we were. It was eleven o'clock in the evening. I have to admit she was a real Southern beauty. Legs up to her neck, beautiful auburn hair and a smile that could tease a large tip out of the most reluctant customer.

We placed our order (or, at least, I did- Gary was too transfixed to speak).

When Sally returned with our meal she made polite conversation.

"Excuse me fo' leestening, but ah heard you' all work at that there skoooowell across the road?"

"We sure do," replied Gary, his eyes rolling around the back of his skull.

"You all wouldn't have any vacancies now would you? Aahm a qualified sports teacher…"

Our eyes lit up (second time).

"As a matter of fact we are looking for a sports teacher. I am the department head and this here is the Principal. Where did you qualify?"

"University of Alabama," replied Sally proudly. Now the 'Crimson tide' (the sports name of the University of Alabama) was certainly known in the deep South. The university churned out American footballers, basketball players and baseball players by the thousands. What it did not churn out was intelligentsia … but we were looking for a P.E. teacher.

I decided that this was not the time for procrastination.

"Be in school at 08:00 sharpish tomorrow morning and we will interview you." I said firmly.

"Sir ahm not shohwer ah kin make it at thaht tahm."

Not a good start, I thought. I was about to cancel the appointment when …

"You see ah don't finish mah shee-yift till gone 2:00 a.m."

Under the influence of alcohol, Alabama's natural beauty and the desperation of finding a suitable teacher in one week I relented.

"Make it 11:00 a.m., and you might not want to show up in those shorts."

"Aahl be there, sir."

What an opportunity for a young graduate. Working in an International school which paid way more than the local state systems and could promise a career travelling the world. Of course, Gary hired Sally (sounds like a movie title). Once Sally had conquered every disease the little kindergartners gave this new recruit, she was a fantastic addition to my staff.

Incident #6 El Terrore Campground

My secretary got the initial call. I was to join the entire subdivision of houses where I lived on a camping weekend. As many of the students lived in the area I could hardly say no. I had not been camping since I was in Italy and had no proper equipment. Eleanor, the kindest secretary in the world, lent me a two man tent, a Boy Scout gas stove and a couple of sleeping bags. I took the bottom of the sofa, stuffed everything into my Jeep Cherokee and left with my nine year old son, for the North Georgia hills. As I had left the office rather late we had been given directions by the camp organiser and I was to join everyone else late one Friday evening. As usual, I was advised not to ask for directions if I got lost but to call one of the organisers,

"With your British accent the local yokels will assume you're gay and these Georgia hill folk don't take too kindle to gays". (I learned later that Georgia hill folk didn't take kindly to Democrats, Catholics, Black people, anyone from out of state, all foreigners, Jews, Poles … need I go on?

With images of movies set in the Deep South ('Delivrance' was the first which came to mind- a violent movie which presented the locals as bucktoothed, incestuous hillbillies shooting every 'foreigner' that moved …) we set off at dawn for 'El Terrore' campground (yes, the clue is in the name). To be honest, I should have turned back when I realised the camping was in a place called 'Hard Labour Creek'.

It was dark when we arrived. The campground entrance barrier was down but there was a small side-path to a wooden shack with a 'RECEPTIO' sign nailed to the doorway. I'm not sure what happened to the 'N' but assumed it had been shot off the sign by some gun-toting ex KKK gang member.

I walked up the three wooden steps to the decking, and my feet creaked with every step. Inside a light came on and an unfamiliar clicking noise was heard behind the door, followed by one word of a thousand syllables,

"Giiiiiyiiiit!" ('git').

I tried to apologise for being late and began to explain I had a reservation with my sub-division.

"Giiiiyiiit off of ma' property."

I retraced my steps back to the path in front of the 'RECEPTIO' building, whereupon the door opened, a shotgun appeared alongside a four hundred year old toothless lady, and I was greeted with the words,

"Now sir, what can ah do fo' y'all at this ungodly tahm o' nhat?"

It was 9:00 p.m. Surely, even God didn't sleep that early?

"Good evening, "(the old lady's eyes lit up on hearing my gay, British, foreign, democrat voting accent), y'all are booked in at plot number 68, assumin' y'all's name is Heel?"

"Thank you, ma'am, I'll just pitch my tent there then."

"You all's gotten a teyent? Rest of youse have about ten RV's hooked up to electricity an' all sorts."

Ah well, welcome to glamping in the USA.

Chapter 4: 1996-1998 Paris, France

1996-1998 World Cup caterpillar and the cemetery trip - Paris

Prologue

Not wanting to have a teenage son in the good old 'U.S. of A' we moved, after the 1996 Olympic games (where I was the Olympic Envoy for Malta-but that's another book) to Paris. Here I took up my second Headship at an American school.

It was humid and hot in the costume. I and a dozen American high school students could hardly breathe. I knew I should have turned down the offer from the French football federation to participate in the opening ceremony of the World Cup, France '98. Unfortunately, my football team insisted. Besides, how many of us get the chance to dress as a caterpillar, whilst lying in wait under an oversized flower, before running around a World Cup football pitch in the opening ceremony?

My wife had just taken a job with FIFA and asked me to organise a team of international students from the American school to assist with the opening ceremony in the brand new Stade Francais in St. Denis, Paris. A dozen hand-picked students were to hide under an oversized flower, inflate it, and then emerge as caterpillars. To this day I have no idea what the connection was with the World Cup. I vaguely remembered a footballer for Wolverhamption Wanderers called Ron Flowers but was sure that was not the link ...

We had thirty seconds to climb under the deflated flower, fill it full of hot air, release its petals and uncover a huge football from its centre into the stadium and then extricate ourselves dressed as caterpillars. Teamwork is instilled into every American student (how else can the educationally challenged footballers gain a scholarship to a U.S. university unless their on-field results are exceptional)? We were competing against ten other flowers in a hot humid Parisian stadium.

The flowers were not the only things we had to inflate. Our lime-green caterpillar costumes contained a small, battery-powered fan which inflated them and made it almost impossible to move under the confines of the flowers. Picture a dozen people under a giant flower, leaf blowers and gas, blown up like oversized sumo wrestlers, trying to manoeuvre a giant football ... A level physics was easier! The entire adventure is captured for posterity on the internet.

KK and the Cemetery

After that first year in Paris I realised that many students left after a one year stint 'doing Paris' and others arrived for their one year tour. One family which is indelibly stamped in my memory was the KK family from the USA. KK was a well-known movie star who had been shooting a movie in Hawaii and was moving to his next movie in Paris. He shipped his wife and kids to Paris directly from Hawaii. So directly, in fact, that they arrived before their bags on a cold, wet, October morning in cold, wet Paris. Mrs. KK brought them directly to school so that she could sort their bags. They were freezing. I loaned them the school track suit and sports gear (easy to do as my wife was the Sports Director) and off we set … on our Halloween trip to Pere Lachaise cemetery. Now, I know what you are asking,

"You took private, International school kids to a cemetery?"

Yes, we did, and a great Halloween trip it was too! The only instruction I received from KK was on my pager, a few minutes before the coach departed.

"Mr. Hill, can you make sure my kids get me a brass rubbing of Jim Morrison's grave?"

Chapter 5: 1998-2014 Antwerp, Belgium

1998-2014: Antwerp Mafia and Sports Day Road Rage- Antwerp, Belgium

Prologue

In 1998 my old boss in Milan invited me to take over from him at a British school in Belgium; my first post as school Director.

In the early days of computer networks, schools could never find anyone with enough knowledge to set up an internet and printing network. The big companies charged obscene prices and there were very few independent small companies. Keen to be the first school in Belgium to have a complete computer network, I found a hippy and a hippy's assistant.

My I.T. hippy of 23 years in age had long hair, smelled of hashish and wore a black suit, black shirt and black tie. He looked like he had just stepped out of a 'Cosa Nostra' movie.

Not only did Hans set up a fantastic network but he also provided twenty second hand computers (of which more later). Hans was a tall, muscular guy with a serious face. He rarely smiled and never divulged any of his personal life to his client; even though we became friendly and ate lunch together after each network visit. Hans was really helpful outside school one day.

We had experienced a number of petty thefts in the street where the school was located. Parents' vehicles if left open at pick up time had handbags stolen, there were several muggings and the street was becoming unsafe. I had reported every incident to the local police but no action was taken.

On this particular morning Hans had invited me to lunch and we had just got into his large, black BMW when I saw a teenager whizzing up and down the street on a moped. He stopped at each vehicle and then accelerated on to the next, peering in at the driver side window each time.

"That's the guy who has been stealing and terrorising the street, and our parents; let's have a chat with him. "

Hans floored the accelerator and bumped the BMW up the pavement at the precise moment the moped passed. The rider was suddenly jammed against the brick wall of the church next door and the BMW passenger door. I can only imagine what the delinquent was thinking as he saw the driver, dressed in black; myself in a dark suit and tie; and both in a large black BMW. I decided to have a word.

"I know you speak English, everyone in Belgium does so listen to this," I said in my best 'I'm going to put you in a concrete overcoat and throw you in the river' voice. "This street is the English mafia, we are here to protect our customers, if you or your mates are seen here again we'll come for you, and your mopeds."

"And your families, and your pets and …"

"Thanks Hans, I think that's enough, we can go now."

Hans put the BMW in reverse, let out the clutch with a scream of the tyres for effect, and we sped to lunch.

We never saw the delinquent, or any of his mates again.

Sports Day at the school was a challenge. Our school served the Indian Diamond exchange in Antwerp and was located in the city. We had no sports facilities whatsoever. A previous Head had negotiated a long term contract to use the fields of the British Fisherman's Association in the Antwerp dock area (Quay # 79 if I remember well).

Unfortunately this meant ferrying (excuse the pun) all the sports equipment in teacher cars all morning to prepare for the big day - the biggest school fundraiser of the year. To make matters worse, about 15 minutes before the relay race I realised we had left the batons back in school. I dived into my car and sped out of the fishermans' playing fields as fast as I could.

As I exited the main gates to the road leading to Quay # 478 (or thereabouts) the cyclist ploughed into my car. I am certain he ploughed into my car and not the other way around. The main reason I am certain of this is that to hit a cyclist with a car in Belgium is practically a capital offence. Crowds will gather round the driver, baying for blood, tying knots in ropes for the eventual lynching and collecting wood for the ceremonial burial burning ... You get the idea. I was, quite literally, pooing my pants as I untangled the mangled heap of metal from my car.

Before the cyclist could say a word, I had bundled him and his racing bike into the back of the car, asked him where his nearest bike repair shop was, demanded his address and informed him that on the way we would be collecting relay batons. The poor guy was still in a state of shock when I dropped his bike off at the shop and him at his house.

Chapter 6: Zug, Switzerland

2008: (I become a school inspector)

Bat droppings and Larks on the Lake - Switzerland

Prologue

During my time in Belgium as Head, Board Chair and practically owner of the school, boredom set in. I needed something different from the same old Headship. I had worked for an International School's advisory body on and off for several years as a consultant and felt the time was right to take some time to travel; paid travel that is.

As a school inspector I could divide my time between being a consultant Head of School in Belgium and visiting schools around the world as an 'Accreditation Officer'.

I already had my own ideas about which countries would have the most organised schools and one of my first 'accreditation' visits was in Switzerland. As a young teacher in Italy I had spent a weekend with a Swiss family in Zug in the early '80's. I knew that every Swiss chalet had a nuclear bunker and the family I was staying with maintained a completely empty bunker under the house. So ... very organised you see?

"Why do you keep it empty? Surely in the event of a nuclear attack you would need food and water?"

"Yes, but then spending weeks underground with a bunch of Swiss would not be my idea of survival," replied the (Swiss) husband.

Still, cleanliness and hygiene, gun polishing and dental repairs on chipped Toblerone teeth were my expectations on arrival in Switzerland. I was disappointed. The school was housed in an old, wooden Swiss chalet, a protected building on Lake Geneva. The library was in the attic. My enthusiastic team of inspectors were due to write the section of their report on school resources so we donned oxygen masks and climbed the four floors to the library.

At the entrance, the carpet was covered in a filthy grey film of what looked like bird shit. Not something we expected to find in sterile Switzerland …

"No, it's not bird droppings," explained the librarian, "it's bat crap."

I checked the school inspection manual- no reference to bat shit. I marked "Fail" on my sheet and proceeded to the Head's office …

"Now about the primary section playground bordering the lake," I began, "surely the little ones can fall in the water, there's no fence?"

Before I could proceed with my fact finding, I noticed a small boy wading into the lake to rescue his football- yes, behind the back of the Headmaster himself and at exactly the moment I posed my question!

"Never happened," replied the Head confidently.

"Turn round," I suggested, marking my school Health and Safety sheet 'Fail'.

Chapter 7: Melbourne, Australia

Casino Capers- Australia

Prologue

One of my duties in school accreditation visits was to train locally based educators in our school inspection protocol.

After one particularly challenging inspection visit the head office, feeling a twinge of guilt, rewarded me with a trip to Australia where I was due to train inspectors and check a few schools with my newly acquired Aussie trainee inspectors. In this particular city, we could not leave without a team visit to its famous casino could we? The school obligingly loaned us their brand new school minibus and off we set.

The parking was underground, down a rather steep ramp. Ignoring the 'Max. Height' signs and buoyed with enthusiasm after what had been a particularly enjoyable visit to state schools in the area, we proceeded slowly to locate a space. Within seconds of entering the car park we heard a screeching and scratching as the concrete roof of the parking deck met the top of the school's (still brand new) minibus. We were stuck. Reversing meant more scratched paintwork, advancing would cause serious dents in the bodywork.

One of the accompanying local inspectors was a big shot in the state educational administration in Western Australia.

"Aw shit mate, we need to lower the suspension, nobody get out. We need more passengers to get in!" After politely asking complete strangers if they would like to spend a few minutes of their valuable time in our company, cramped inside a school minibus, the suspension was lowered sufficiently for us to reverse and get out. But what were we to do about the scratch marks on the roof of the vehicle?

"It's white, look I'll just get one of me mates to Tippex over the marks, the Tippex will set like concrete in this heat." So we did.

A few years later I met the Head of the school in Egypt- he had been so enthused with our visit that he decided to further his career in an English school in Cairo. He did, of course, remind me of the school's generosity in lending the mini bus for some local "sightseeing"... I confessed to the whole story and like a true Australian he saw the funny side!

Chapter 8: Netherlands

Mostly the Moat, fire drills and other short tales - Netherlands

Prologue

The Netherlands has a reputation for having a caring and relaxed attitude in schools. My experience on one school inspection certainly confirmed that.

My team and I had been informed that the school was run by the state but in partnership with the Church, a common practice in the Netherlands. This particular school was notorious for taking students who were unable to follow traditional education and needed English. Many had been expelled from other International, British and American schools in the Netherlands.

Our impression on arrival was quite favourable. The school was housed in a large chateau (once used by the gestapo in WW2 we were told). The building was beautiful. The original owners had bequeathed the school to be used only as an educational foundation. The drive to the chateau was impressive: lawns, a lake and a moat surrounded the building.

As we approached the large, oak doors we heard music from within. Someone was treating us to a medley of Coldplay and Elton John numbers on the piano.

Inside was a rather dishevelled student, who greeted us and politely answered all of our initial questions.

"Do you do this every morning or is this especially for us?"

"Every morning, and all day."

"All day?"

"Yes, I don't go to classes, I'm too much trouble"

Students filed into school, knocking their backpacks against what appeared to be paintings by Rembrandt, Rubens etc "Surely not?" I asked myself ...

The school was a boarding school, so as per our usual schedule of inspection we announced that we would pull the fire alarm on Day 2 of our week's visit.

"No you won't", announced the school receptionist. "This is a protected building, National trust you see, nothing is allowed on the walls. No wiring, no alarms, no nothing. However, we do have a system of air horns ... "

"Air horns?"

"Yes, look there in the bottom drawer, we press one and then someone in the next section of the school sets the next one off and so on."

"But if they're all in the bottom drawer?"

"Er, yes good point ... I suppose we should give them out?"

"Yes please, by 10:00 a.m. tomorrow".

The next day at precisely 10:00 a.m. I stood by the receptionist who was holding the air horn rather too close to her right ear.

"You might want to hold that at arm's length," I suggested.

"Why is it loud?"

"Well it was the last time I heard one at Anfield," I answered. Needless to say, I marked "Fail" on the 'Effective Fire Drill systems' on my report. However, we still had not yet tested the boarding house…

The following day we used the air horns both in school and in the boarding accommodation block. We had asked the standard procedural question, "Is everyone accounted for?" and had been met with the response, "Absolutely!" from the Head as the entire school lined up in front of us. Oddly though, we could see all eyes turned slightly towards the left and behind us. An older pupil, Walkman playing, earphones plugged in, and head bowed was approaching the neatly assembled lines of staff and pupils. As we turned to face him, he looked up, mouthed "Oh f..k!" and joined his class.

Boarding section evacuation plan: 'Fail'

With the school failing its inspection in a variety of areas, we thought we had better check the staffing provision in the boarding house during the evening. Boarding schools tend to operate a skeleton staff evenings and weekends. I sent our most experienced inspection team member, an American sports coach, to the chateau around 7 pm on the third day.

"You won't believe what I saw!"

"Oh I think I will-do go on."

"You know the moat? Well as I arrived I could see all the boarders lined up around it in a circle. I could hear them shouting, "Swim, swim, swim!"

"What?"

"Yes, when I asked that guy who plays the piano in the entrance what was going on he told me it was the initiation ceremony for the new kids". They were swimming in the moat, one full tour of the chateau, chased by some of the largest pike fish I have ever seen."

All this seemed par for the course for this school; or so I thought…

The science labs were housed in old Nissan huts behind the main school block. Science classes are crucial to an understanding of a school's attitude to laboratory safety protocols and undergo stringent safety inspections. The chemistry lab was rather cramped. We noticed that underneath the makeshift sinks (sunk into ordinary wooden school desks and already somewhat of a fire hazard), were plastic tubes and buckets.

"What are those for?" I enquired with a feeling of dread.

"Chemical waste. We can't have that emptying into the school plumbing system can we?" responded the chemistry teacher.

"… and what happens when the bucket is full? Where is it emptied? No, don't tell me ."

The image in my head was of the new boy swimming in the moat

I marked, "Laboratory safety protocols - Fail"

Chapter 9: Riga, Latvia

Kitchen Chaos- Riga, Latvia

Prologue

Several months after Latvia gained its independence from Russia I was sent to inspect and accredit the country's first post-Soviet-era private International School. The school had been hastily founded by the U.S., British, French and German embassies in order to provide an English education for the first expats from those countries keen to trade with this new Baltic State. International schools are quite often a barometer for a nation's economic progress.

The new school campus only extended to one end of the old agricultural college building. A well-lit international school corridor with plush lighting and modern heating abruptly changed to a dimly lit freezing cold concierge's office. This was where the Soviet era college began. The stark contrast between East and West, and this new 'Iron Curtain' where two worlds met was both enlightening and depressing at the same time. The old Soviet concierge was still sitting at his 'welcome' desk in the gloomy atrium. Perhaps no one told him that Latvia was now, well, Latvian …

The first American Head of the school had warned my team that there was only one hotel, one taxi and practically only one road in the capital, Riga; (wide enough to accommodate Russian tanks of course). The school was housed in an old Soviet agricultural college and educational supplies were provided by the U.S. embassy.

Riga's one hotel was freezing. We burned hard copies of our draft inspection reports in the meeting room fire to keep warm. The hotel manager was convinced we were from the I.M.F. and looked after us very well indeed!

Breakfast was whatever the kitchen staff could find and, not wanting to be too demanding, I ordered an egg on my first morning.

I wondered if an egg was too complicated … but,

""I find," replied the waiter with a smile.

The omelette arrived and I proceeded to order exactly the same for the next three days on the grounds that anything else might be too difficult to obtain. On day four there was an almighty commotion in the kitchen, pots and pans were hurled and I could hear the waiter shouting.

Moments later my waiter appeared - no omelette.

"I sorry- but chicken, he stolen last night," he explained.

On arrival at the agricultural college the next morning (after a 5 km per hour taxi drive) we set up our team room. As soon as we switched on our computers the school fuses blew. The caretaker (let's call him Boris- why not?) arrived. He had his testing gear - a light bulb and two wires. Boris proceeded to open the fuse box and took out a bottle of vodka. After a large swig he touched the ends of the two wires of his bulb "multi-meter tester" at various points across the fuses. We heard a bang and saw a flash as Boris was catapulted back onto the stone floor.

"I find!" he announced proudly and a few moments later the lights came back on.

Chapter 10: Astana, Kazakhstan

"You will die!"- Gin & tonic, icicles, skiing and Kazakh police- Kazakhstan

Prologue

Our inspection teams were divided regionally around the world. As I was based in France it made sense to give me responsibility for schools in Europe and Eurasia.

Flying into Almaty airport is always fraught with difficulty. For several months of the year it is covered in fog. At other times it is -40 degrees centigrade.

Not long after Kazakhstan broke free from Soviet dominance and declared independence, a series of tri-lingual (Russian/Kazakh/English) schools were established and as a result inspection visits were frequent. On this particular visit my plane was rerouted due to fog to from Almaty (the old Soviet capital) to the new capital, Astana, where we landed at 01:00 a.m.

Not wanting to spend all night in a Kazakh airport in the middle of the Russian steppes in winter, and with only a faint knowledge of Eurasian geography I asked the helpful police officer (resplendent in his Soviet style uniform with the curled peaked hat) if I could hire a car and drive to Almaty.

"No- you are going to die."

"What?"

"You will die"

I had experienced some poor hospitality on my travels but the threat of immediate death was not something I had anticipated. Why were they going to have me killed? What had I done? I had not even had time to mark "Fail" on my report. I had not even set foot in their government school.

"Why?"

"Is minus 40 degrees, no one leaves Astana in car, so cold you will die."

That made more sense.

I arrived in Almaty the next day to a balmy -26C. I spent two days in a delightful school and returned to Astana. Winter in Kazakhstan was interesting. Thick carpets were frozen to the pavements outside the hotels and restaurants to avoid slipping, cars had electric blankets plugged into the cigarette lighters and the wind pierced all forms of western clothing. Undeterred, I and my inspector colleague from Boston USA, went down to the hotel bar for a drink.

"Two gin and tonics please."

"Da! Gin tonic, I bring."

Our glasses arrived. Warm glasses, warm gin and warm tonics. Clearly refrigerators had not yet arrived in the new capital.

"Any chance we could get some ice please?"

"Niet. Is no ice here."

I looked outside, there were at least six inches of ice glued to the pavement. I gesticulated a spade and shovel movement,

"Perhaps you can get some outside?"

The barman laughed, he seemed to communicate that digging solid ice was not part of his totalitarian work contract. We gave up.

The following day was our first school visit. We were met at the hotel by the American Head of School and his caretaker driver. Like many people in Kazakhstan the driver was a former policeman and had also worked on the site of the Soyuz' space programme's headquarters as a maintenance engineer. Stalin in his infinite wisdom had sent all the political dissident members of the intelligentsia as far away from Moscow as he could. This created a super intelligent elite among the families living in Kazakhstan and Boris the driver was clearly more than just a school driver/caretaker.

On our way to school we were stopped by a police officer with a peaked Soviet style hat again- only this time with quite a few medals on his large chest. Boris explained that we were going to get a ticket for making an illegal turn. This seemed odd as almost all roads in and out of the city were as straight as a ruler.

"Of course if you don't want ticket, you can pay him," suggested Boris.

The American Headmaster was livid. This suggestion of police corruption was too much for him on his first assignment out of Ohio.

"Are you kidding? I'm not giving him a cent, I'd rather go to jail!"

"I wouldn't," I replied firmly, "I have a job to do- I'll give him twenty bucks." I handed Boris the money but the officer proceeded to write a ticket anyway.

"See?" said the Head, "I warned you."

"No," said Boris, "he pretend write ticket, no marks on paper, police camera on wire above head, we ok."

Sure enough, the policeman handed the blank ticket through the window.

I immediately took advantage of this situation. My son was a musician in a band in the UK. He had a penchant for ridiculous hats.

"Boris, ask him how much he wants for his Soviet police hat, I want one."

A few minutes later, and after much bartering and emptying of pockets (mine and thirty dollars) the officer wrote a name on a piece of paper.

"He tell me … we go find man in main market …I go for you before you leave," said Boris helpfully.

"That's thirty dollars wasted," said the overly cynical American Head.

Later that day I thanked Boris as he showed us the school's buildings and grounds. He was particularly keen to keep pointing at the tiny icicles, hanging from the corner of each gutter at various locations on campus. The icicles were constantly melting and dripping water- despite the -26 degrees.

"What is it Boris?"

"Last inspector - stupid American- he say health hazard, icicle big as a sword. Fall on children then cut off head. I put electric wire and attach to plug- he melts and now safe for children."

I marked on my inspection report, 'Health and Safety - Passed'.

I had forgotten about my thirty dollar Kazakh police hat until I arrived at departures in the airport on my way home. The customs officer, on seeing my passport, waved me to an office to have it stamped. There on the desk was a large plastic sheet, like those you see at the dry cleaners. Not only had Boris sorted the hat, but a complete Kazakh police uniform!

I marked *'Attitude to Visitors'* on my school inspection form: 'Passed, with flying colours'

I neglect to mention the American Head's accommodation. While life for International School Heads may be challenging at times, the salary (almost always tax free) and the accommodation often made life much easier. Not so in Almaty, or so it seemed. The Head of this school invited me for dinner and a sleep before my 2:00 a.m. flight. His apartment was in an old Soviet bloc. Grey, dismal looking concrete with an elevator which had not been in use since the Cuban crisis. The newly independent and wealthy Kazak middle class nouveau riches had time and money for a new car (Range Rovers were everywhere) but luxurious apartments were still under construction. Even so this school was really saving the dollars; the apartment was awful and not something which would attract a top quality Head of School from the U.S.

The next day I interviewed the charming school Board Chair; an affable Indian business man who had a pipeline construction company. He asked me for suggestions as to how he could continue to assure the future of his school for the expatriate community.

"You might start with improving staff accommodation, beginning with your Head of school," I suggested.

"What? He has a brand new apartment at the foot of Chimbulak ski resort."

I had seen these magnificent, new apartments from the taxi on my way, with our man from Boston, on a day's skiing over the weekend (more of this later in this chapter).

"Er no, his place is horrible. Fourth floor, no working elevator, ancient furniture."

"No, first floor, gardens, pool, modern Ikea stuff."

It later transpired that I had uncovered a scandal. The Head was paying for his daughter's education by renting out his new apartment to a Kazakh oligarch and living in a shithole. Before I finished my report back in the office at home he had been summarily dismissed.

Chapter 11: Taipei, Taiwan

Taiwan Taster - Taipei

Prologue

For some strange reason, Taiwan was later added to my European regional responsibility. As an inspector (actually, the more fancied term was 'Accreditation Officer') for an International schools' group I would often inspect or train school staff to prepare for their inspection or to use the correct terminology an 'Accreditation Visit'. Presumably this phrase was used to take the heat out of the word 'inspection'.

I arrived in Taiwan before Graham, the inspector from Australia. Just outside the hotel was a line of lively bars and other less salubrious establishments (a.k.a strip joints). Imagine my delight to find that 'Charley's Bar' served British Boddington's beer from the then Strangeways brewery. (A little known fact at the time, and very appropriate, was that Strangeways was the Manchester prison).

"What you want, American?"

"I am definitely not American, British, and call me Andy"

"O.K. Mr. Andy, what you want?"

"I'll have a Boddingtons and a burger please."

"Body and burger for Mr Andy please, chop chop quickeee!"

The following evening, Graham arrived. I suggested we ate at Charley's.

"Ah, welcome Mr. Andy, Boddington's and a burger for two, yes?"

"Blimey," said Graham, "are you sure this is your first visit to Taiwan?"

Contrast this with the Italian restaurant we went to the next evening (after being told specifically by the school bursar not to go to any expat restaurant - a tip that, as volunteer inspectors, we ignored). A two hour wait for the meal only to be told that there was no chef…

Before leaving for Taiwan my Belgian accountant had asked me to collect as many "VAT style" receipts as I could for the annual VAT returns. Company tax was less than personal income tax so company income was always offset as much as possible.

I gladly returned home with one large receipt, a bill for 300 GBP equivalent in Taiwanese currency. Tom, my accountant, was less happy,

"I'm not sure the VAT man in Brussels (my home at the time) will accept this receipt at 03:00 a.m. from the "Happy Dancing" restaurant on a Sunday morning."

Chapter 12: San Jose, Costa Rica

Volcanic paradise-San Jose - Costa Rica

Prologue

You might be forgiven for thinking that the international school inspection trail seems like a large number of jolly trips to exotic places ... I don't blame you; most of the time it was. Occasionally, however, we were rewarded with some very exotic locations outside of our allocated region.

Costa Rica is a beautiful country, it really does have everything, flora, fauna, two oceans, no military, and a British school founded I think by a couple of backpackers (or so the rumours went).

The flight from Madrid ended in near disaster at U.S. immigration in Miami. I had spent four years in Atlanta, where I obtained my green card and then left to return to Europe. This was my first trip back. As I entered customs I made a bad decision. To avoid the queues I went through the area marked 'Resident Aliens and Green Card Holders'. I have always been intrigued by the term, 'Resident Aliens', often expecting to see an area rather like the bar scene in 'Star Wars', complete with weird monsters, "Welcome to the United States Mr. Momaw Nadon, Zutton, and Ponda Baba."

"Welcome home Mr. Hill ... only the U.S. is no longer your home is it? Do you still hold a bank account in the U.S.?"

"Well, no."

"Have you declared taxes in the last three years?"

"Er, not exactly."

"We are going to have to ask you to surrender your Green Card then."

"What? Mexicans shoot each other for Green Cards and you want me to voluntarily surrender mine?"

"Step this way sir."

My only option was to comply. I signed the form.

"Thank you sir, as you have arrived on an International flight I imagine you have drunk alcohol?"

"Too damn right, er I mean yes."

"Then can you sign this waiver form confirming you are sober and able to surrender the Green Card?"

"But if I sign the form saying I am sober I could be drunk?"

"One minute sir, I hadn't thought of that."

(A few minutes later)

"Sir you will need to remain with us for 4 hours, then sign the forms again."

I called the Head of the school in Costa Rica to inform him I would arrive late around 01:00 in the morning. He collected me from the airport, or at least tried to; two flat tyres on the school minibus, with the Head of school changing them (in a new suit to impress the inspector) and two hours later I made it to the hotel. I marked my report in advance, "Health and Safety: Fail"

Monday morning saw the inspection team introductions during the school assembly. I had done a little homework and knew the following Saturday was the local football derby between Saprissa F.C. and Liga F.C. and was looking forward to the game. I had managed a "Good Morning" in front of the entire school assembly when the heavens opened on the tin roof of the assembly hall. No-one caught a word of my well prepared speech, not a word, nada.

As if to emulate Norman Collier's famous broken microphone sketch I mimed the speech and waited for the rain to stop. At the precise moment the deafening noise stopped I shouted, "… to see Saprissa!!!!". The Saprissa supporters in the student body went wild! That broke the ice.

i) An American's first 'soccer' match:

I had worked with 'tricky Ricky' on inspection teams many times before. Rick was a jovial chap from the East Coast (who eventually bought his own local bar in Madrid-but that's another story). I decided that as a reward for his work I would treat him to a football game, the biggest in Costa Rica- the local derby! Despite living in Madrid for years Rick had never experienced a single match.

As we approached the stadium, with crowds gathering enthusiastically Rick asked if I had the tickets.

"Not yet."

"Where's the ticket office?"

"No idea, but one of these people here will have tickets."

I could see the concept of a ticket tout was too un-American for Rick, he looked very uncomfortable.

I caught the attention of a policeman on his horse, "Where do I get two tickets for the match today?"

The policeman looked at a large, plump lady and held up two fingers, "Signora, gringos, dos!"

I paid in U.S. dollars, and the lady handed a few to the policeman, "Gracias!" she said to him. Everyone was happy. The policeman got his commission, the tout received her over- inflated price and we had our seats. Rick was appalled.

"But he's a police officer!" he wailed indignantly.

"Yup," I replied, welcome to Central America!

Our 'seats' were lumps of concrete behind the goal, in the middle of the Saprissa section. As we arrived I explained why I had chosen places just in front of the crush barrier.

"When Saprissa scores, the crowd will surge forward and we won't be crushed," I explained enthusiastically. Rick was appalled, again.

"Is this safe?"

"No idea mate, but it's as safe as I remember as a child back home on the Kop in Liverpool."

We were surrounded by families eating bread rolls, offering us meat and rice and the atmosphere was both friendly and electric. This changed suddenly the moment the opposition team came out onto the pitch. Any nearby fans supporting Liga were treated to an assortment of spitting and shouts of "Puta" (I'll let you check out the translation for yourself).

The 'Cueva del Monstruo' ('The Monster's Cave') stadium was transformed from a family-friendly sports arena to a Roman amphitheatre where there could only be one winner.

Rick endured the event and I think actually enjoyed it, despite being an American, a gringo, knowing nothing about 'soccer' and still wearing his school inspector suit.

ii) **Pompeii in Costa Rica**

If you have never been to Costa Rica I highly recommend it, this beautiful country really has everything for the tourist. At the end of our inspection visit my team of six went to the hot volcanic springs, of which there are many in Costa Rica.

As we all stood drinking gin and tonic, and listening to the Australian inspector's reasons as to why the Australian dollar notes are waterproof (you can guess why) we looked at the red glow of the Irazú volcano in the distance. I had recently been to Pompeii and was enthusing about it when Rick planted a vision in our heads.

"Imagine if the volcano erupts now. We'll all be perfectly preserved in our school inspector bathing costumes, our gin and tonic glasses in our hands standing in a perfect circle toasting the success of the school. A thousand years from now the International Schools' Accreditation service will have some questions to answer when they excavate our bodies from the volcanic ash."

A beautiful vision indeed …

Chapter 13: Cairo, Egypt

Egyptian Record breakers - Cairo

Prologue

After several inspections I had clearly convinced Head Office that I was up for almost anything...

Cairo is one of my favourite cities. I have always been drawn to cities with an air of chaos in the streets and on the roads. I love Istanbul for example, and New York. If I have learned anything about living and working abroad it is to lose some of those British ways and act like a local-I love doing this. I like to jump the queue in Italy, buy fake clothes in Istanbul markets, and I even enjoy the so-called rudeness of New Yorkers (more about New York later).

Even the dozens of International, British, American and French schools in Cairo have an air of chaos about them. Still, all this is compensated by wonderful Egyptian hospitality, the food, and their enthusiasm for sport which is unparalleled in the Middle East.

As I approached the grounds in the first of many school visits I decided, as often was the case, to do the facilities health and safety check first. By and large Egyptian expat schools have wonderful campuses with amazing facilities, particularly sports stadia. This particular school was no exception. Indeed the running track was a brand new 'Mondo Rubber' professional, Olympic standard track.

Outside the sports hall was a list of the school's athletes and their successful times in local competitions. As I looked at the list I could not help marvelling at the 400m records.

As a keen follower of most sports I have in my head that the average time for a high school male runner in a 400-metre race is about 54 seconds and 58 seconds for females of that age group. For the average student off the streets, 70 to 90 seconds would be an average time, with elite runners running between 45 and 47 seconds. The notice board listed a lot of 44 second times!

I managed to corner the Head of P.E. who explained why the times were so quick.

"We had the track built over the holidays and there was no one to check the construction. Our caretaker oversaw everything and was certain the track was laid at 400m. When he questioned this on completion it turned out that some of the Mondo Rubber surface disappeared between delivery and laying ... about 20 metres!"

"So it is in fact, 380 metres?"

"Er ... thereabouts," replied the Sports Director vaguely. "I reckon the school caretaker has a super soft play area in his back garden."

I marked the 'Facilities' section of my report, "Inadequate".

Chapter 14: U.A.E.

Fastest zebra crossing in the world-UAE

Prologue

The Middle East and the UAE in particular hosted a rapidly expanding network of International Schools and the region was added to my portfolio later in my career.

Inspecting schools across the Middle East is often fraught with surprises. Sitting with a school board across the table from the Sheikh's wife (one of the many I presumed) can be quite nerve wracking for both parties. Many school systems in the UAE rely on a successful inspection in order to increase their fees (it is forbidden to do so prior to a successful inspection). As a result there is a lot riding on the week's accreditation visit.

The first few minutes of one such week did not go well. As usual my team arrived early to check the safety procedures during student arrival and drop off. This was the time of day when health and safety were often at their tightest (e.g. 'carpool'' in the U.S.) or when child safety was thrown out of the window... or even when an overly eager father threw a child out of the window ...

For instance, in this particular school...

The Indian parking attendant was waving his arms in the air like some kind of deranged octopus. Cars were arriving in the car park from all directions. There were no lanes or lines and children evacuated cars, dodging other vehicles and ducked under the arms of the deranged octopus. There were no assigned parking spaces and cars moved off in all directions once they had emptied their contents. Children, mothers and bodyguards spewed out of the vehicles and ran for the safety of the school entrance.

I marked "H and S-Fail" on my report and called an emergency Board meeting.

The school Board, in the presence of just one member (yes, you guessed it the sheikh's wife) had already explained the loss of a few million dollars in the annual budget.

"That would be the new swimming pool," explained the accountant to Mrs. Sheikh.

"... and how did we pay for that?"

"Er ... well that would have been your donation maam," explained the accountant.

This meeting was a little more serious. Child safety is at the forefront of all school inspections. I described the scene we had witnessed earlier and Mrs. Sheikh was horrified.

"Does this mean we have failed the accreditation inspection Mr. Hill?"

"Well, unless things improve by tomorrow morning, yes," I replied rather nervously. Pictures of my hand being chopped off, or worse entered my head.

"See to it," Mrs. Sheikh looked squarely at the Head of school.

The following morning I held an emergency meeting of my inspection team.

"Remember that child safety is the first and most important standard a school must meet, so let's not worry about our body parts finishing up in a sandy hole in the desert," I quipped.

We needn't have worried. As we arrived at the drop off area in front of the school a large zebra crossing had been painted across a new tarmac area. It was equipped with flashing lights. A one way system had been introduced and the deranged octopus was as happy as Larry (or Mohammed).

Mrs. Sheikh had joined us to survey the scene.

"I expect this means we will pass the inspection and the increase in fees will pay for these improvements?" she asked.

"Certainly ma'am," I replied. Visions of body parts dropping aimlessly into wicker baskets disappeared from my thoughts.

Chapter 15: Dublin, Ireland

Down and Out in Dublin-Ireland

Prologue

During my time as an International School Accreditation officer I worked as a consultant on various school projects. One such project was to 'save' a down and out school in Dublin.

'Down and Out' because it had recently closed due to financial constraints. One such constraint being that the school had very few students, and not all the parents paid fees on time, if at all. In fact, it was difficult to see how parents paid their fees, the invoicing and issuing of receipts was haphazard to say the least. My consultant business partner and I were invited to look at the school, with a view to a buyout or potential merger with other successful schools.

It was too late. We arrived at the beautiful campus, situated next to an even more beautiful golf course to see a school in complete disarray. The swimming pool was green with slime and mould, and a tour of the kitchens left us horrified. The school had been abandoned overnight. Food was left in the refrigerators, and tables were set for a meal. The classrooms were equally messy. Chairs and tables all over the place, books covering the floor. Our guide, a locally born sponsor and fund raiser who had built a number of classrooms in the school's more successful past, was horrified. He was an alumni and had supported the school after achieving a very successful music career with one particular romantic hit which was number one in ten European countries.

After a close scrutiny of the accounts a few days earlier, we upset the guy further by informing that the last expenditure of any note was a load of musical instruments- none of which we could locate in the school on our tour. Keen to show us the beautiful castle-like campus in detail, our musical guide seemed to be particularly proud of the building's towers and pigeon lofts. So proud, in fact, that he insisted on taking us up an old, wooden, spiral staircase to the pigeon tower. As I followed behind him he asked if I could give him a shove. I placed a firm hand on his buttocks and shoved with all my might. The intimacy of this incident was lost on the man, but will remain an indelible stain on my memory. My embarrassment knew no bounds and my face went as red as the lady's dress in his one hit wondrous song!

Chapter 16: Monaco

2012-2014 Bodyguards guns and knives - Monaco

Prologue

After far too many years travelling around the world I was offered another permanent position.

Bodyguard number 1

It makes sense that oligarchs and middle-eastern leaders are careful with their offspring. Monaco has the most public video cameras in the world and the fact that the Chief of police' daughter was the kindergarten assistant should also help keep the little ones safe. A school in Monaco has to be extra watchful over the parents, bodyguards and children in its care. So when a driver entered the building, brushing me aside to reveal a handgun under his jacket, I had to take action.

"Sir, may I speak with you for a moment?"

"Da, first I deliver child to classroom."

"Er, no you will not, I'll get the assistant to do that, you are coming to my office.

One of the things which makes being an International School Headmaster really interesting is how sections of society still bow their heads, show puerile fear and become really nervous when called into your office. This bodyguard was no exception.

"Have a seat. Now, I cannot allow you to enter my school with a handgun under your jacket."

"Niet, but how I say child is safe? No I must, my boss he say…"

"Tell your boss that if you enter my school again with a gun the Chief of Police will have his papers confiscated and he will return home immediately. My assistant will meet your vehicle by the roadside and walk the girl into school."

"Da, I go now please?" (I could see being in the Head's office evoked bad memories for this giant of a man).

"Off you go, run along then," (I just couldn't resist saying that).

Bodyguard number 2

One middle-eastern parent felt it safer to live on his yacht in the harbour rather than in a Monagasque apartment (probably cheaper to be honest). His daughter had never been on a school trip but as she was now reaching the end of Primary school he decided to allow her to go for a week in the French mountains with her year group.

"On two conditions Mr Hill. One, that you accompany the children with the teachers and two, that my daughter's three bodyguards go with her."

"Three?"

"Yes, one will be there but you will never see him, one will always be visible and close, and one will take part in all your activities. They are all ex Royal Marines, except the fourth …"

"I thought you said three?"

"Ah yes, but the fourth is not mine; she is supplied by the French security services."

"Agreed."

I mean, what could happen in the Alpes Maritimes on a school hike and nature walk?

Well … the aforementioned French bodyguard clearly was not interested in guarding a child. On the first day's walk she told me she had been the actor Alain Delon's bodyguard. (Strange that the handsome, womanising Alain had chosen this particular brute.) To make matters worse, walking up the mountain with a bunch of noisy Primary school children was, in her opinion, rather demeaning and not a great career move. The lack of action bored the poor woman to tears, until …

The Mercedes turned the corner just as we had blocked the road to walk the children across. As usual we stopped the traffic in both directions, teachers and myself arms outstretched as the children walked safely between us. The Mercedes was in a hurry and we saw no sign of it slowing down. Believe it or not, drivers often do this when children cross the road as if to say, 'You lot stop and let me pass, then you can cross, this is my road."

We held our arms out, confident the car would eventually slow down. It did not appear to… At the last minute, the French bodyguard shouted,

"Arrête, attendez vous monsieur".

As if to make a point the driver slowed to a crawl, continuing to advance towards the children. Before the Royal Marines could swing into action, (there was definitely a camouflaged rustling in the bushes by the roadside), our French "garde de corps personnel" pulled out the largest fishing knife I had ever seen, jagged teeth, rusty face (no not the bodyguard, the knife… although …) and leaped on the bonnet of the Mercedez, knife in one hand, with her official protection I.D. in the other and pushed both up against the windscreen shouting,

"Je vous ai dit d'arrêter la voiture monsieur!"

The driver turned pink, his wife burst into tears and I would not be surprised if the driver's seat might have needed a deep clean in the morning.

Chapter 17: 2014 - 2016 Kuwait City, Kuwait

2014-2016: Kuwaiti Arrest Warrant, leaking loos and medical supplies ban-Kuwait City

Prologue

In 2014 my sense of adventure and desire to pay off our mortgage got the better of me. I took up an emergency Headship in a challenging school in Kuwait. 'Challenging' because the previous three Heads had all done a bunk without fulfilling their contracts...

Part 1 In jail (or nearly)

"Are you Mr. Hill?" demanded the Kuwaiti police Colonel.

"Officer, since you came directly to my office from reception, you must have seen my name on the door. How may I help you?"

"Well actually we are arresting everyone without immigration papers in your school today. Perhaps you noticed we have arrested a number of your Bangladeshi cleaning staff?"

I had of course noticed police rounding up my school cleaners and positioning them, hands behind their backs, in a sitting position in the playground. They looked terrified.

"Colonel, please sit, have a cup of tea. Now, how do you know the school has yet to process my papers?"

"One of your ex teachers informed us."

"Would that be the lady I fired yesterday for passing exam photocopies to a GCSE student she was tutoring?"

"Probably, in any case we need your passport for a few days".

"No chance, my passport stays with me. What's the alternative Colonel?"

"You come with us and the cleaners to the police station."

"Fine, can I take my car?"

"Yes, follow us."

"Perfect, only don't drive like a maniac …"

Forty five minutes later I found myself in the Colonel's office at the police station in downtown Kuwait City. I could see he was uncomfortable with this 'arrest'. After all, we Brits had saved Kuwait from the Iraqi National Guard a few years earlier during the first Gulf conflict and Kuwaitis were incredibly hospitable towards British expats.

"Tea?

"Yes please.

"Turkish delight?

"How kind"

"Mr. Andy, you do not look concerned …"

"Well, the way I see it, the school lawyer will contact the Sheikh and I'll be out of here in no time. Alternatively, you deport me, so I get to keep my return flight money from my contract- it's win-win really".

"Are you British always so calm?"

'Well Colonel, on a scale of 1-10 compared with everything else that's happened to me in my career this is a 4."

The Colonel smiled, he seemed disappointed.

"But someone will be made to pay Mr. Hill."

"Who would that be?"

"Your History teacher, he's on his way here now, he also has no papers, we are deporting him this afternoon. "

I called Gary and immediately informed him- he was actually quite pleased as he already had a new job in Jordan and was going home a month early with cash in hand.

"Another Turkish delight Mr. Andy?"

"Too kind, thank you."

Sure enough, a few hours later the Sheikh's lawyer arrived to bail me out and I returned to the end-of-year staff breakfast at the Hilton. The teachers already knew I had been arrested and cheered when I showed up armed with Turkish delights and a big smile on my face.

Part 2- Leaking toilets and medical supply ban

You may think it never rains in Kuwait but you'd be wrong. When it rains it absolutely chucks it down. The rain washes sand into the drains and … well, suffice to say that the school playground/concrete football pitch/break time play area definitely had insufficient drainage. Worse still, all three areas were actually one, with up to 1800 students using the facility daily.

The enthusiasm of the break time footballers knew no bounds. Not even a flooded 'pitch', nor a mysterious brown sludge emanating from the toilet block could stop football.

This play area was so congested at break times that there were frequent accidents- a football kicked in the face at point blank range, a clash of heads, a scraping of knee skin etc. In order to save money one of the sheikh directors banned the use of medicines at break times.

"But sir," I pleaded, "we have hundreds of kids out there running around- there's bound to be accidents."

"Headmaster, from today absolutely no running at break times- see to it immediately!"

Honestly, you could write a book …

Part 3-Towels in the Hotel

One week after taking up my post as Deputy Headteacher, the Head was fired. It seems he had allowed some more liberal families to collect money for a graduation 'party'. On hearing the word 'party' the Sheikh owner fired the Head and I was instantly promoted. The promotion allowed me to move out of my school apartment and into a pleasant, family run Hotel ten minutes from the Marina and five from the beach. I loved the place. The Bangladeshi staff were super friendly, as were the reception staff- though both seemed to be totally disorganised. I have often reflected on why whole nations produce populations of totally disorganised peoples. Is it something in the genes? The water? Is it the heat? Look at Southern France, Southern Italy, the whole of S. America (except Argentina which is only disorganised in finance), and Kuwait. Let me give you my classic Kuwaiti story.

Kuwait is populated mostly by expats who outnumber Kuwaitis 5:1. Kuwaitis themselves are super friendly, super polite and super helpful and super disorganised. For example, the beach road along the gulf had just been replanted with palm trees. This should eventually provide shade, greenery and beauty to a dusty, dirty beach road. But no. The trees were saplings a few centimetres high and once duly planted, were never watered and quickly died. I could imagine the conversation in the Ministry of Palm Trees in downtown Kuwait city. (There was a ministry for everything in Kuwait so I feel safe in asserting that a 'Ministry of Palm Trees' probably existed):

"But boss, the trees were all planted like you instructed!"

"Did I suggest you plant tiny trees no higher than my toes?"

"To be honest, you did not issue any direct height instructions."

"And the water?"

"What water?"

"The irrigation you idiot, where is the water to grow the trees into a magnificent tree-lined avenue of which our glorious leader can be proud- may he receive all the blessings of our God?"

"I received no instructions about water, despite the wishes of our glorious Sheikh, may he live a long life."

"Okay, but how to fix this for his glorious eminence?"

"I will immediately plant bigger trees and irrigate the avenue, Minister."

"Excellent."

"For a few hundred thousand Dinars of his glorious highness' money."

Let's get back to the towels…

My hotel was busy at the weekend. Saudi guests came over the border into Kuwait to shop and go to the cinema. This put a strain on the hotel's organisational abilities every Thursday evening (the 'weekend' being Friday/Saturday). The Reception was exceptionally busy during Thursday evening, made even busier by my presence.

"Aah Mr. Andy, how can we help?"

"I need clean towels please."

"That will be difficult as we are very full …"

"Yes," I interrupted, "but you took the old ones away and now I have none."

"We will solve that immediately, Abdullah will bring your towels."

By the time I had returned to my room, the towels had been placed in the bathroom.

"Wow!" I thought, that's unusually efficient!"

Except it wasn't. The towels were still wet. I grabbed them and headed to Reception.

"Aah Mr. Andy, I see you have your towels!"

As I summoned up my best British sarcasm I felt the breath of the Kuwaiti hotel owner behind me, which might have explained the receptionist's nervous demeanour. I ploughed on regardless.

"Mr. Ahmed, what are towels for?"

"Well, for drying the body Mr. Andy."

"So not for wetting the body then? Are towels ever used for that?"

"Er no,"

"These new towels are wet, ergo, they are not towels are they?"

"Er, let me see what we can do," (nervous looks towards the owner as Ahmed picked up the phone."

A few minutes and lots of shouting later.

"Mr. Andy, we have no more towels in the hotel, you see we are very full."

(More sarcasm in my voice).

"I am delighted you are full, that's great business, I bet your owner is really happy, and would be even happier if you were full every night, what do you think?"

Ahmed could not divert his eyes from the owner who was now shuffling his feet and coughing loudly behind me.

"Er, yes, Mr. Andy."

"So are you telling me that you would rather the hotel was never full so that you can save money on towels?"

At this point the owner behind me intervened, whispered something in Ahmed's ear and Ahmed disappeared across the road to the Filipino supermarket, emerging a few minutes later with a pile of new towels.

I thanked Ahmed, whereupon the owner asked me if I would like to fill out the form in the suggestion box. Despite me explaining that I had already made my complaint and received my towels, he insisted. I wrote, 'Buy more towels, fill hotel every night, give Ahmed a pay rise- Mr. Andy room # 12."

Part 4 - Christmas Police

My hotel lobby had been decorated … with a Christmas tree. I was really surprised, Kuwait being quite a traditional Islamic country. At school we had recently shipped out a teacher within 24 hours of him 'accidentally' throwing a book at a student. The book was the Koran. My more loyal students warned me that there might be a riot in school if I did not act swiftly.

I did. My S.African Maths teacher was out of the country within eight hours. I had learned rather quickly that being a guest in another country meant just that. Act like a guest, be as polite as a guest and never criticise your host. During Ramadan I did not eat or drink at school, and I did not drink water in my car at the traffic lights. Imagine my shock, then, upon seeing the Xmas tree in the hotel lobby.

It was a beautiful tree. It was a tastefully decorated tree. It had silver lights and gifts at the bottom of its trunk. I was asked by the receptionist if I objected to having a tree in the lobby. I learned that Ahmed asked as many guests as he saw. Clearly he did not ask everyone though. A week after the tree's installation two Kuwaiti policemen arrived, packed the tree into their patrol car and sped off into the dust (or sand).

The two officers were the Xmas police. Their job was to identify any offending examples of religious artefacts on display which might offend the official religion of the country.

In my head to this day I imagine being interviewed by the Captain of Police for this exciting job:

"So, why are you interested in being a Xmas policeman?"

"Well, firstly, I like the work hours. I'm really looking for a seasonal job you see and this one's very seasonal isn't it?"

"It certainly is, a couple of weeks in December is all!"

"… and I like to travel, will I see much of Kuwait?"

"Well, only the international hotels, but on the bright side, they are all on the beach."

"So great for the lunch breaks then. Is it safe being a Xmas police officer? Will I need to be armed?"

"Hardly, you will be dealing with expats employed here, if they cause any trouble we revoke their work visa, so remember to mention that should any expat cause a rumpus."

Chapter 18: 2016-2018 London, U.K.

2016-2018: 'Vive La France'- London

Prologue

After Kuwait I took a temporary Headship in a school in central London. The school had a large majority of French expatriate families and was bilingual (French /English).

<u>The Ofsted Inspector's pants</u>

I am proud to admit that in over forty years of involvement in Education, I had never experienced an Ofsted (Office for Standards in Education, a U.K. government fish tank, oops, *think* tank) inspection. International schools abroad mostly use their own model. An international school accreditation is much more collegial, with a team of teachers from all over the world spending a week in school looking for the positives; not just the 'let's see if we can trip them up' negative style of British inspections.

The school had a large majority of French expatriate families who cycled (across Regent's park), walked and scootered to campus each morning. The French kids were waved goodbye by their parents,

"Travaillez bien", ('work hard', and the Americans would arrive a little later,

"Have fun!" (There is a cultural message on the importance of education for some countries there).

The fun stopped when Ofsted announced an inspection. In fact, everything stopped. There were frantic messages from school owners to unearth documents on attendance, health and safety, building regulations and frankly anything that had little or no connection with the education of the students. The owner of the school was in finance. He was a benevolent man who had needed a new interest after selling his business.

"When is the Ofsted guy coming?" he asked me.

"Tomorrow," I replied nervously.

"Tomorrow, why such late notice?"

"They only give notice the evening before, we heard at 6:00 p.m."

"Bastards," judged the owner.

The following day the Ofsted team of three arrived. The Chief Inspector was a very large chap. He looked like a model for a doughnut house; one of those on a pole outside the doughnut place. Indeed, his eyes lit up in a similar way when he saw our beautiful school building.

"This place is super."

"Yes, do you speak French by the way?" I asked.

"No, not a word."

"Well done Ofsted," I thought, a French school being inspected by a leader with no French at all.

The school had a lot of stairs. My office was on the 4th floor. "Serves you right," I thought as I watched the inspector wobble up the steps, clutching the handrail as if it would save his life in the event of a fall. The steps were unevenly built and at different heights. Some were quite a challenge. Not a challenge mastered by the inspector. As he stepped up to one of the higher steps I heard a rip. A tear in his pants. A tear in the bottom of his pants. A tear so large I caught a glimpse of fatty, pink flesh poking out of what had been his rear pocket. Suppressing an involuntary movement in my throat I ignored the noise and the sight. So did the inspector.

As soon as he was able to sit down in my office he confessed.

"I've torn my pants and I do not have another pair."

"Not to worry, Oxford Street is just round the corner. Give 'em your size and I'll send the receptionist. She's from Paris and has an eye for fashion." ('Which obviously you do not', I thought as I scrutinised his torn trousers.

Needless to say, at the end of the week and before we knew the result of the inspection I presented the chap with a receipt for the new trousers. He nearly had a heart attack when he saw the amount.

"Seems a little expensive?" he questioned.

"Fashion, class and quality have their price," I answered.

<u>Police anti-terrorist squad learns francais</u>

Twice a day we walked the students to Regent's Park, our playground. (The school was housed in a beautiful Georgian building in a mews near the BBC). It was no mean task taking over a hundred kids at a time across 12 busy roads and past the Chinese embassy, through traffic and armed guards. The armed guards were posted outside the Chinese embassy. Flak jackets and heavy machine guns held high. Each break time the French kids would greet the guards,

"Bonjour monsieur,"

"Bonjour, vous allez bien"

Etc.

The anti-terrorist squad would look inquisitively at our students muttering,

"F …..g frogs" etc.

Chapter 19: 2018-2021 Central West Africa

2018-2021: Snakes in a School, ... and on a plane - Central West Africa

Prologue

After London I had officially retired, or so I thought. You might think that retirement to our beautiful home in the hillside above Cannes, swimming pool and all would be the dream end to a glittering career. - I added 'glittering' but if you have read thus far you really cannot disagree can you?

Just as I was getting bored with the high life I received a call on my mobile phone and to this day I have no idea how she got my number.

"Mr. Hill?" (A female voice with a heavy but unusual French accent).

"Yes, speaking?"

"I am the private secretary of the First Lady of ..." (somewhere in Central West Africa), "We want you to help the International school, founded by the First Lady but now in some difficulty, can you come for an interview in London tomorrow?"

Never being one to pass up a free trip I quickly agreed and after an interesting interview with the First Lady, her bodyguard and the tea boy (who I later learned on arrival in Central West Africa was a major investor in the school) was offered a contract. It seems the school had had five Heads in four years and needed an older, experienced and unflappable chap like myself if it was to progress further.

A few weeks into the job and,

"Comme les lapins Monsieur le Directeur!"

"What do you mean they're like rabbits? Snakes are nothing like rabbits!"

"I mean, like rabbits, they are everywhere in 'zis country!"

He was right of course. In the tropical regions of Central West Africa snakes are everywhere. But you don't really expect to find them in a school, not even in Africa.

I had already experienced snake protocol during a visit to Australia as a school inspector. I remembered watching the children play a traditional non-violent children's game (Aussie Rules football...) and had noticed a ditch around the field. It seemed dangerous; surely the children would fall and have an accident?

"Aw shit mate, look, that's to keep the bloody snakes off campus!" the school grounds man explained.

But this was different, this was in tropical Africa, this was in school.

I knew something was afoot when I arrived on campus that morning. As usual, my shirt and suit jacket were already soaked at the back. I had never really worked out how to dress as a Headmaster in the tropics. My business manager told me to wear a vest under my shirt to hide the sweat marks but that just seemed to increase my body temperature. It was hot, humid and horrible. But a walk around one of the world's most beautiful campuses, with its small stream, palms, kingfishers and lizards usually cheered my spirits. The lizards bobbed their heads up and down to greet me, as they did outside the school reception building every morning. But this morning was different. Instead of lizards there were secretaries, four local administrative staff quivering, not bobbing, outside the main entrance doors.

Helpfully, the French parent representative had warned me of snakes on campus on my first day on the job; black and green mambas-both deadly poisonous.

"You need to get to the hospital super vite for the antidote."

"Just as well that the private hospital is across the street then?"

"Yes, but they never have the antidote …" was the comforting reply.

But on this particular morning the office staff greeted me with,

"Monsieur, a snake, a snake!"

"Where is it?"

"In the uniform shop!"

Admittedly, the thought of a green mamba staging some kind of anti-uniform protest did strike me as unlikely but a venomous serpent cuddling up in the cosy warmth of a school jacket pocket was quite probable.

Snakes are deaf, so no amount of hysterical screaming from the locals was likely to frighten them. Our snake expert, affectionately known as the 'snake charmer of Cameroon' had told us to stamp our feet and it would run away. It took a good deal of stamping around the uniform shop before the administrative staff (and parents) set foot in there again I can tell you.

We were of course well trained in dealing with such incidents. A few weeks earlier the snake charmer of Cameroon had been invited to educate us in how to deal with snakes on campus. Our PTA had organised a presentation for staff and parents and another for students. However, I had not foreseen that he would actually bring his own snakes, in a suitcase and on the plane from his native Cameroon! Equally unforeseen by the flight attendants I imagine was the fact that he put the suitcase in his carry-on luggage. Yes, carry-on luggage!

Chapter 20: Central West Africa (cont.)

"Police, Papers please!"- Central West Africa (continued).

Let me state here and now that almost everyone living in Africa needs money to feed their immediate family, provide medicines for their children and care for their extended families. In Central West Africa France still receives money into its national bank from "former" French colonies. I use the word "former" with reservation. Many of these countries are monopolised by French businesses, French supermarkets, French airlines (well one to be exact), French food and for those using the Central African franc ("CFA") even their currency is pegged to the Euro. There are gendarmeries stationed in capital cities, military uniforms are French with local labels attached with velcro and even the street signs are the same as any you would find in Paris.

As a result of all of the above, life is expensive. Local police add to their monthly income by taking cash whenever they can. This could be quite alarming for expatriates such as myself, but I saw it as an amusing challenge, a way of life and tried to behave as locals would when stopped and asked for driving documents. Below are just a few examples of the situations in which I found myself over a three year period.

Incident # 1- School Car Impounded

As a newly arrived Head of School I do rely on employees who know the country better than I, usually Deputies, Bursars, Board members.

My Bursar was showing me the way to the beautiful beaches, an hour's drive from school and from the capital city. Just outside the airport he explained that as wealthy looking expats in a company 4x4 vehicle we would almost certainly be stopped.

We were.

Two policemen demanded passports, (duly provided and checked), driving licences-some confusion here as mine was not a local one and did not match my passport, (duly provided and checked), and finally vehicle insurance (duly provided, checked and found to be out of date …).

Just to remind you, I was travelling with the one person responsible for the aforementioned insurance documents; the Bursar. After a long discussion, a Captain arrived and impounded the car which we were forced to drive to the airport pound. Strangely though, the 'airport car pound' was directly in front of the Captain's office.

"Cent milles s'il vous plaît".

"Is that the fine for recovering my car?"

"Beh, oui ..."

"I have only 50 000 ..."

"Ça va, 50 000" alors.

I handed over the notes, and waited for the fine and receipt. No fine, no receipt, just the car keys. I think I was beginning to understand how to play this game ...

Incident # 2 - School car clamped.

I am convinced there are only two clamps in the whole of Central West Africa. I was clamped by both of them (not at the same time of course). In the centre of the capital, Libreville, was an area known as 'petit Dubai'. It could not have looked less than Dubai. It was really a shopping area for appliances, furniture, kitchen utensils and washing products. Every shop was owned and run by the Lebanese community, who also had a monopoly on restaurants and beach hotels. The Lebanese are incredibly business minded. Let's face it, how many times have they rebuilt Beirut?

I parked my car outside one such shop and within seconds my eye caught the blur of a man running towards my door. Clamp! My front tyre was immobilised.

"What do I do now?"

"Police precinct, Room 13B, pay" was the subtle response.

I took a taxi. I took two taxis in three years during my stay; largely because the drivers would steer violently to the left while the car made its own decision to veer right, or the brakes would deafen any conversation inside the vehicle, or the taxi emitted a black smoke the reason for which I could not never work out-though I assumed the diesel was watered down with palm oil.I

"Do you mind if I pick up other passengers on the way?"

"Will I pay less?"

"Non"

The police precinct was a scary place. In the entrance hall was a large cage, and inside this makeshift prison were those arrested the night before who were unfortunate not to have any cash on them to bribe their way out. Men, women, teenagers huddled together-most without water.

"Room 13B?"

"A droite, deuxième porte, petite porte, très petite porte"

I walked down the hallway, looking for some miniature door. 13, 13A, tiny unlabelled door, 13C

I knocked on the tiny, unlabelled door and walked in. Sitting behind a small school desk was a police officer with no Velcro number on his shoulder-local police often did this to avoid official complaints by members of the public.

I handed over the piece of scribbled paper the clamper had given me.

"100 000", demanded the officer.

This time I was ready.

"I only have 40 000, it's Saturday, I need the rest for my beer while I watch my football team."

"Paris St Germain?"

"No chance, Liverpool!"

"Vous n'êtes pas français?"

"No English"

"OK 40 000 seulement pour les anglais, 100 000 pour les français!"

I wondered if the two tier fine system was embedded in local law …

Incident #3- Police Chase in school car

'Police chase' may be a slight exaggeration as you will learn below. After being stopped a number of times I had asked a Board member for advice. I was told that if there was no police vehicle or

Velcro officer number in sight, that the policeman was off duty, so I could simply ignore the police and drive on.

On this particular evening I was on my way to take my car to the car wash and had been stopped twice already. Clearly the sight of a well-dressed expat in a 4x4 was still a magnet for local law enforcement. This third spot check occurred within 100 metres of the first two. I saw no police car, so ignored the policeman's outstretched hand and simply drove past him.

Pleased with myself I pulled up at the next set of traffic lights and was about to set off when, with a screech of brakes, a taxi pulled up in front of me blocking the road ahead. Before I had a chance to scream, "What the f… do you think you're doing?" a police officer jumped out of the taxi. Yes, the same one I had ignored minutes earlier.

"You were trying to escape."

"Trust me, if I wanted to escape I could have run faster than your taxi!"

"Permis de conduire svp." (Driving licence please).

As usual I locked all the doors, closed the windows and pressed my licence up against the window, explaining that I had already been stopped by this guy's mates only 100- metres away. I also used the same story I often used.

"You do not want to fine me or impound my car. I work for the President's family (sort of true as the First Lady founded the school). I will lose my job, and you will lose yours."

This almost always worked ... *almost* always.

<u>Incident # 4 - Covid Curfew and England v Italy Euro finals</u>

During the pandemic, Central West Africa was incredibly well organised and put most wealthy European countries to shame. Covid tests were mandatory for all airport arrivals and departures and there was a Covid check for all passengers, with quarantine while they awaited their results. A curfew was applied (from 09:00 p.m. till 06:00 a.m.) and police with military vehicles were stationed everywhere. Bars were closed. Sort of ...

I had been watching the England v Italy game; extra time and penalties took it to well past 09:00 pm. I drove very slowly home but rounded a corner and was confronted with military vehicles (not the usual Velcro-stripped local cops).

"It is past curfew- why are you driving? Do you have an emergency?"

"Absolutely, I have to go home and throw some plates against my kitchen wall and scream at anyone I see!" (Yes, I assure you I literally did say this, in French of course).

"Pourquoi?"

"England just lost …"

"You are not French?"

"No, see my England top and my Stevie Gerrard signed shirt which I wear for luck!"

"That didn't work then did it?"

"Er no,"

"I mean it definitely did not work, 50 000 CFA s'il vous plait!"

I never questioned the military police, too frightening, and handed over the money.

Incident #5 Coup D'état

Four in the morning, in tropical Central West Africa. This was my usual time to switch on the air conditioning after the heat of the night but something was wrong. I imagined I heard helicopters outside and rolled back to sleep. There it was again, more helicopters.

Staff accommodation was not far from the government buildings in the city centre and the main beachfront highway which lead to them. The helicopters were circling and soon the phone calls came in, Bursar, teachers, admin staff, board members.

"Keep your radio on, make all your calls now, there will be no internet soon," was the advice.

"Stay in the staff accommodation till further notice, there is an attempted coup."

Indeed, a lowly lieutenant in the Central West African army had taken over the radio station (quite a bizarre plan as almost no-one listened to national radio) and announced a military takeover, to the surprise of the entire population and to the even greater surprise of the military ...)

A military takeover announced at 4 a.m. was perhaps indicative of the organisational capacity of those in charge of the coup.

My wife called first. She had heard the news on the BBC and consequently knew more about what was going on from our home in France than I did in Central West Africa.

"How's things?"

"Great, we all have a day off confined to quarters."

"Can you get a taxi to the beach?" (My wife knew me well).

"Seems not, the government is preventing mass demonstrations by having the police stop every taxi and forcing the driver to hand over the car battery." (Only in Africa could this piece of ingenious demo-breaking work so well).

"Do you have supplies?"

"Yes, I have water purification tablets, bread, cans of food and most importantly gin and tonic."

"No sweat then, catch you later," replied my wife-stoic as usual.

In fact the coup lasted a day. A week later the four military culprits were paraded on the national news by their captors, the French army (hard to believe that the local military were not involved, yet another sign of French colonialism still at work..).

Incident #6 Real Housewives

The country's authorities handled the Covid Pandemic admirably. Strict curfews with roadblocks were enforced, all incoming flight passengers had to undergo mandatory Covid tests on arrival at the airport in the capital, and Libreville taxi drivers were obliged to wear masks (handkerchiefs mostly) and gloves (often old gardening gloves).

Bars and restaurants enforced strict mask wearing (at least on entry and on exit) and Libreville's city beach was closed to prevent too much mingling.

Two employee wives seemed to be oblivious to these rules. It was around 7:00 p.m. when my bursar and I received the call. Two of our teachers' wives had been arrested exiting a beach bar without a mask. We learned later that everyone exited the beach bars without masks but these two were caught. It was clear that one of the 'Real Housewives' was upset. We could hear the wailing. Without hesitation (well, actually after some considerable dialogue e.g.

"Should we go and help?" "They're not strictly our employees."

In the interests of P.R., we jumped into the car and sped to the beach- five minutes away.

We must have looked imposing to the arresting officers. Two white men in suits and ties in 100% humidity was not a frequent sight. I sensed a certain amount of indecisiveness as we arrived.

"These two ladies must accompany us in the truck to the police station," insisted the braver of the two Beach Police Officers. Yes, Central West Africa has a 'beach police', 'police des plages' and yes, it must be a great job …

The bursar, addressing the Beach Police, waded in (excuse the pun):

"There is no way these ladies are getting in the back of a truck full of drunken men and frightened teenagers," he insisted.

Beach police officers often left their charges in the trucks for hours until parents or friends showed up to pay the "fine".

"Then we will take them in the police car."

"No, that's not going to happen either. We will take them to the police station ourselves, you can follow."

"How do we know you won't escape?" demanded the braver of the two arresting officers.

"Well, you can come in the car with us."

We set off, two employees, two real housewives of Central West Africa, a Bursar, a Head of School and a police officer.

Before I describe events at the police headquarters I need to add some background. Our Bursar was well known at the police station (he was well connected everywhere in the country). Incidents of trespassers hunting birds in the school grounds, a drunken officer ploughing into the concrete pillars of the school entrance and a colonel mysteriously winning our 45+ tennis tournament at the age of 40 were all well-documented at police HQ.

Indeed, when we were all martialled (excuse the pun again) into the colonel's office his heart sank, his face dropped and he let out a heavy sigh.

"Bonjour Messieurs les Directeurs de L'école."

"Bonjour Colonel"

The colonel turned to the arresting officers, his look said,

"You have dropped me in the shit now … there's no way we can arrest these two expatriate citizens but they have broken the law, what the hell am I supposed to do with them?"

Sensing the Colonel's torment we offered a solution.

"Colonel, fine the ladies, and we will be on our way. Furthermore we will initiate training for employee's wives on the Covid laws."

We knew there was no way the Colonel could risk any paperwork involving two prestigious expats (not the housewives but myself and the bursar). The bursar, ingenious as always in the face of local laws, suggested we might pay the fine directly to the officers. We left the Colonel's office, settled the 'fines' in cash and publicly admonished the Real Housewives loud enough for the Colonel to hear.

Chapter 21: 2021 Northants, U.K.

Full circle- back in Northants U.K.

Prologue

After forty years abroad, my family and I decided to return to the UK. Brexit made living in France problematic, and I was ready for retirement. Or so I thought.

After a few days in the Northamptonshire countryside watching daytime television, I gave up on retirement, found a teacher supply agency and was offered multiple opportunities as a temporary teacher on substitute supply. I was anticipating a big difference between International students and homegrown British ones but I was not prepared for a return to a largely broken education system.

My first assignment was for two days in a 'Good' High school in a rural village. On arrival, the Department head of English slung a walkie-talkie around my neck and informed me that if things became difficult I was to press button one, whereupon someone from the 'corridor police' would intervene and collect the student(s) concerned.

The 'corridor police' (that was the nickname I used) were the discipline department (pastoral teachers is the official term- a group of teachers out to pasture was, indeed, a fitting term for them …).

As I lined up my first class outside the main door I could hear murmurings of,

"F..k me he's old!"

"Look at his hair!"

"What's your name, granddad?" All this from the teenage girls.

I lasted a day. Hats off to all those state school teachers teaching bottom set Year 10 fifteen year olds ... it's a zoo out there. Thank you to the British government who invented the National Curriculum so that disaffected, uninterested, mobile telephone-wielding teenagers are forced to study Macbeth, Charles Dickens and awful reality plays from Liverpool.

I tried a different school in the village of Doctor Martens. (Not to be confused with the 'Doc Martin' television series which is set in an idyllic village in Cornwall). This was the village of Doctor Marten boots; the boot factory was situated near the school and opposite the glue factory. Thinking about it, that glue factory would have been handy for the school's pupils in the seventies when glue sniffing was all the rage...

I lasted two terms, largely due to a fantastically well-organised English department and my new approach: teach the one third who wanted to learn and ignore the rest. That way, no-one told me to, "f...k off" or tried to burn my desk. The nicer kids only tried to vape in class, and as long as I interjected every lesson with football stories they let me live.

Personal, Social and Health Education classes were a hoot. My group of very mature fifteen year olds told me in no uncertain terms they were not going to participate. They had seen it all before and in any case, as one boy noted,

"There's no slides on heterosexual activity sir, just people committing suicide, gettin' sexually transmitted diseases and LGBTQueens Park Rangers".

"Okay," I countered, "here's the deal. You keep a paper on your desk, numbers 1-10 in the margin. Then you can fiddle with your phones till the corridor police arrive. When the door opens-Brian will have given us the signal in advance- I will start question number 1. It's as if we were starting a test on the LGBTQ slides, see?"

"Genius sir! That's sick!"

"What's the warm up question?" asked Brian. Brian was a slightly intellectually challenged (bit thick) footballer.

"I will ask you Brian, this question:

'Should a professional footballer have sex before an F.A. Cup final?'

"Brilliant sir!" Brian paused for a minute, deep in thought, or as deep in thought as Brian could ever be.

"Sir?"

"Yes, Brian?"

"What's the answer then?"

At the time of writing I am gainfully employed as an English teacher in a school football academy and I love it. I teach International students who play high level football and occasionally attend classes when there is no training or matches. I dare say I will add to the anecdotes already penned above as my new retirement career enfolds....

Manufactured by Amazon.ca
Bolton, ON